Bea,

Trust in the Lord!'

Psalm 37

Fear Not! I am with you.

A journey into God's plan for fearless living.

Pastor Tim

by
Rev. Timothy Sternberg

All Bible quotations not translated by the author are from the:

The Holy Bible, English Standard Version® (ESV®)
Copyright © 2001 by Crossway,
a publishing ministry of Good News Publishers.
All rights reserved.
ESV Text Edition: 2007

The fear of the LORD is the beginning of wisdom, and the knowledge of the Holy One is understanding.

Solomon, circa 1000 B.C.
as recorded in:
"The proverbs of Solomon, son of David, king of Israel"
chapter 9, verse 10

Fear Not! I am with you.

INTRODUCTION

The phrase, "Fear not!" is widely believed to occur 365 times in the Bible. While that number is exaggerated, the phrase is written a remarkably great number of times – a fact that always made me wonder, "Why?"

Fear is very often said to be a bad or an unwanted emotion. "The only thing to fear is fear itself!" "Don't be afraid!" "You are such a scaredy-cat." Sometimes, though, fear is suggested as being worthwhile if it keeps us out of trouble. "A little fear is a good thing." "He was afraid of being hit so he ducked."

The fact that God tells us to "Fear not!" so many times, combined with our tendency to think of fear as a negative feeling, led me to believe that when I studied all of God's "Fear not!" statements in the Bible I would indeed find that fear was bad; so bad that we needed constant reminders to stop being afraid.

I was wrong.

(And I'm not afraid to admit it!)

As I journeyed through the Bible, and as I encourage you to follow me along the same path with these devotions, I found that fear is very human and very normal. There are very scary, evil and fearful people, events and ideas which we encounter in life. There is nothing wrong in being afraid of these. We are fragile beings – we damage easily (both physically and emotionally), we fail constantly, we live a brief existence. There is nothing wrong in feeling afraid when we face our own mortality and weaknesses (assuming we do not wallow in these fears).

However, and in Biblical language we would say, ***Behold!***, God appears in the middle of our fears with his word and his command, "Fear not!" It is a bold word of God, spoken to a broken and fearing human being. But it is also a word which brings up many questions – questions to which God has answers.

Question: "Fear not? – Really? – How? How are we to not fear?"
Answer: By trusting God.

Question: "Why should I not be afraid now?"
Answer: Because God is with you.

Question: "What is there to convince us not to fear?"
Answer: God himself. His very nature, power, authority, and past performance.

Question: "Where shall we go to escape our weaknesses and the evil surrounding us?"
Answer: You shall go to God who is your strength and your shield.

These were my honest questions to which God provided clear, helpful, and hopeful answers. God also provided through his many "Fear Not!" statements a vision of and perspective on fearless living. It is my sincere hope that in these devotionals and Bible studies you too will discover the answers and desire of God. It is my heartfelt prayer that study and reflection on all of God's "Fear not!" commands will bring you His peace, a peace that passes all understanding.

Easter 2012

NOTES ABOUT THIS BOOK

– A note about your Bible. Feel free to read any Bible translation (not paraphrase) with these devotions. Different Bibles, though, may have slightly different wording, such as "Do not be afraid." instead of the more literal, "Fear not!" Each "Fear not!" in this devotional is translated from the Hebrew (אַל־תִּירָא) and Greek (μὴ φοβοῦ).

– A note about the Scripture readings. It is _very important_ to read the Scriptures before the devotionals, not only because Scripture is paramount, but because many devotionals may not make sense until seen in the context of the Scriptures upon which they are based.

– A note about the quotes from the church fathers. At the end of many devotions are quotes from the early church fathers. These men are like grandfathers or great-grandfathers who left hand-written letters behind. Their writings contain wisdom and insight, humor and culture, passion and piety. They are a treasure chest which many people never open. I hope you enjoy just a few brief excerpts.

– A note about the Bible studies. Most often a Bible study that is based upon a thematic or topical idea runs along the lines of, "Here's all the instances of (.....insert theme or topic.....) in the Bible. Let's look at them and see how they apply to or impact our lives." The Bible studies of "Fear not! I am with you." are different. Titled, **Diving In**, these studies are contextual and theological.

A contextual Bible study takes you on a journey to understand the context of each occurrence of "Fear not!" in the Bible. Sometimes this means looking at instances of 'God's Spirit' in the Bible to get a better understanding of what God means by saying, "My Spirit remains among you. Fear not!" Sometimes it means examining the structure of a passage as in Joshua 1. Sometimes it means illustrating a Biblical person's life to see how fear was a part of their relationships. This Bible study is also theological. In truth, all good Bible studies are theological because they are a study in God's (theos) word (logos). In this study relevant and important teachings of the Bible are explained simply and clearly.

Together, the contextual study and theological teachings serve one goal – to develop a deeper and more meaningful relationship between you and your Creator. As when lovers spend time together walking and talking, so too will you share in the wonderful life which God has prepared for you.

1

Genesis 15:1 "Fear not, Abram, I am your shield."

Read first: Genesis 15:1-6

This is the first instance of God saying, "Fear not!" in the Bible. It is not the first occurrence of fear however – that happens in Genesis 3:10 when Adam admits to God that he was 'afraid' because he was naked when he heard the sound of God walking in the garden.

One of the interesting elements in Genesis 15:1 is that the man to whom God speaks does not appear to have anything to fear at the moment; although he has experienced much recently which would cause many a courageous man to fear. In chapter 12, Abram is told to leave home and travel to an undisclosed location. Later his wife Sarai is abducted by Pharaoh and still later he faces a civil war of sorts between himself and his nephew Lot. After giving the best of the land to Lot and taking his chances with what is left, Abram was told his nephew had been taken captive by the armies of four kings. Now, while the unjust abduction of a loved one is enough to strike fear in many of us, Abram gathered a small army of his own and attacked – certainly a heart pounding endeavor – and defeated the four kings and rescued Lot.

It was "after these things" the Bible says, that God comes to Abram to tell him to, "Fear not!" Wow! What could possibly cause this man to fear? If he was unafraid in the face of the unknown, in the face of a haughty ruler, in the face of family strife, in the face of aggressive military forces, what does God know, or what does he foresee, that Abram will (or should) fear?

The conversation which follows 15:1 is about children and God's promise of children. "Fear not," God tells Abram, "for I am your shield." What does God's protection have to do with having children? Everything! While it is Abram who brings up the child topic, it is God who reveals that his offspring will be slaves for four hundred years. That revelation is surely something to fear – four *hundred* years of affliction in a foreign country, four *hundred* years of your descendants suffering year after year. Makes one almost want to be childless. Almost. But not quite because it is the One who gives the child who also says, "Fear not!"

So what is he, or what are we, to not fear? The future? The fulfilled promises of God? God is Abram's – and our – shield. He is our protection; not from affliction but in the middle of affliction. He does not promise 'no evil'; he promises deliverance from evil. Evil in the future is real and not to be feared because it is powerless to penetrate the shield of God which protects his children.

Prayer: Talk with your Father in heaven about your fears, fears of evil and affliction.

Diving In

"This is the first instance of God saying, 'Fear not!' in the Bible. It is not the first occurrence of fear however – that happens in Genesis 3:10 when Adam admits to God that he was 'afraid' because he was naked when he heard the sound of God walking in the garden."

Question

1. What is Adam afraid of? Is it his nakedness in front of Eve or is it his nakedness in front of God?
2. Is Adam afraid of God's disappointment or God's just punishment? Adam had every reason to be afraid of God's just punishment – death.
3. Why did Adam and Eve both cover themselves? Were they attempting to hide – something or from someone?
4. Why didn't God say, "Fear not!" to Adam?

Theology

The fear of the Lord has a two-fold understanding. On the one hand there is respect. See Proverbs 9:10 and Acts 9:31. On the other hand there is terror of the punishment for offenses against God which carries the sentence of death (which is eternal separation from God). See Joel 2:11 and Revelation 6:15-17. We will look at many more Bible passages on this teaching.

"One of the interesting elements in Genesis 15:1 is that the man to whom God speaks does not appear to have anything to fear at the moment; although he has experienced much recently which would cause many a courageous man to fear."

Question

1. Might Abram be afraid of the voice of God – as is the case with Manoah in Judges 13 and Isaiah in the sixth chapter of his book? Answer: This is very unlikely. This verse records the fourth or fifth time God has spoken to Abram.

Theology

The voice of God can be a very frightening sound. Consider the children of Israel at Mt. Sinai and the disciples on the mountain where Jesus shone like lightning. See Exodus 19, 20:18:21 and Matthew 17:5-6. In the unveiled God (perhaps we may say un-muted), we are shown the holiness which would consume us as a raging fire. In the person of Jesus Christ, however, there is no such fear. The Christmas hymn, "Hark the Herald Angels Sing" says it so eloquently, " . . . Veiled in flesh the Godhead see, Hail the incarnate Deity, Pleased as man with man to dwell, Jesus our Emmanuel." God, in Jesus Christ (as God in similar fashion spoke through Moses), speaks in a tone/volume which we can endure – at least as far as our saved human nature allows us. For those who are not saved because they reject God, his voice is both strident and condemning.

"Fear not," God tells Abram, "for I am your shield."

Question

1. What is a shield? For what purpose is it constructed and used?
2. Why would God use this military tool to describe himself? Obviously he uses it so that we may begin to comprehend an aspect of God – but which aspect?

Theology

God as shield is an image used in the Psalms. Consider Psalm 3:3, 18:2, 84:11, 119:114. Psalm 84:11 is a most interesting passage where God is called both sun and shield. Might this suggest that God is both the light and the one who shields us from his light that we may not die? Consider Moses being hid in the cleft of the rock and covered by the hand of God so that when God passed by Moses would not die!

"So what is he, or what are we, to not fear? The future?"

Question

1. What are you afraid of? Honestly. Make a list. Consider both earthly and spiritual things. Don't be embarrassed to make a list. Fear is natural, human, normal. In listing you may find that some things you are afraid of are silly. On the other hand you may find that there are some things you need to give over to God for his care.

2

Genesis 21:17 "What troubles you, Hagar? Fear not, for God has heard the voice of the boy where he is."

Read first: Genesis 21:8-20

Hagar had much to fear. This was the second, and last, time she was expelled from the home and tribe of Abram. She was wandering homeless, defenseless, and now waterless in the wilderness. She had her young son with her who apparently was dehydrated and near death. What's to fear? Perhaps the better question is, "What is not to fear?!" She leaves her son in the shade of a bush and walks away so she does not have to watch him die. She weeps aloud. Certainly the bitter end is very near for them both.

Then an angel speaks to her, with the sort of innocence only an angel can muster, and asks, "What, Hagar?" (The word 'ails' or 'troubles' is not in the original Hebrew.) What indeed! Only from the perspective of God's providence, power and protection can one look at these circumstances and say, "What of them?"

What is remarkable about this instance of the phrase, "Fear not!" is how the story has been set up for us. It has all been about Hagar, her work, her feelings, her fears. Then God comes and says,

"Fear not for I have heard the voice of the boy where he is." God heard the *boy*. So much for thinking it is all about Hagar. So much for Hagar thinking about herself. So much for ... us ... when we are hungry, poor, defenseless.

Maybe it is not always about us, after all. God says, "Fear not!" because you are a small part of the bigger plan. And since God is in total control of the larger puzzle, he also manages the small pieces. We are not often privileged, as Hagar was, to know the greater plan. The lesson we learn is that our plights are part of the great tapestry God has woven to reveal his great love and salvation. Knowing this, perhaps we should not be afraid we have become an insignificant detail to God and trust that he sees all, knows all, and controls all.

Prayer: Talk to your Father in heaven about your ailments, your pains, and seek His peace about His greater plan for you.

> "Godliness adds length of life; and the fear of the Lord adds days. As, then, the days are a portion of life in its progress, so also fear is the beginning of love, becoming by development faith, then love. But it is not as I fear and hate a wild beast (since fear is twofold) that I fear the Father, whom I fear and love at once."
> – Clement of Alexandria, Miscellanies, ca. 200 A.D.

Diving In

"Then an angel speaks to her, with the sort of innocence only an angel can muster."

Question

1. Angels have a sense of innocence about them. It is almost an oblivious sense in that there are times they seem completely unaware of the obvious. In the case of Hagar, the angel seems unaware that the impending death of her son (at least from her eyes) should be at all distressing. Consider Genesis 16:8 and Acts 1:11. What are the angels seemingly unaware of in each case?
2. How does an angelic viewpoint or perspective help us to see our world, our lives, our mysteries?
3. What do the angels see which we do not? Consider Daniel 10:13.

Theology

An in depth look at angels is beyond the scope of this Bible study. However, it is a fact that angels are messengers and that they brought God's message of "Fear not!" to God's people. God is not beyond sending his angels today to speak words of comfort, encouragement, wisdom and peace. The way we know if we have heard from God through an angel is if what the angel has said is in agreement with what has already been written in the Scripture. Consider Paul's strong statement about angelic messages in Galatians 1:8.

(The word 'ails' or 'troubles' is included in some Bible translations but is not in the original Hebrew.)

Question

1. Why is it that there are words in our Bibles which are not in the original Hebrew? Answer: The translators of the Bible (Hebrew and Greek scholars) do their best to make the English sound correct to the English reader. The same practice holds true if we translate English to French or French to Russian. Sometimes extra words are put in because that is how the language naturally flows. Two words in French might need three in English to make sense as when "bon appétit" means "Enjoy your meal." What is important about checking the original languages is that sometimes the extra words (or words left out) convey meanings which are unintentional on the part of the translators.

Theology

So can we trust our Bible? The answer is yes, especially if it is a widely used translation. If a Bible is a paraphrase, there is a great deal more liberality used when writing and therefore a great deal more caution should be used when reading. In a more technical sense, the Christian church confesses that the Bible is inerrant in its original manuscripts.

Since we have such reliable and numerous (thousands and thousands) copies of the original manuscripts, there is no reason at all to have anything but the fullest trust in the Bible translations which are widely used in the church.

A person who can read the original languages does not have a different Bible to read, nor do they have any special knowledge revealed to them through that skill. They do enjoy a deeper and fuller sense of God's word, however, and because of this they are often moved to preach and teach God's people the joys of God's salvation in Christ Jesus.

"God heard the boy."

Question
1. Who was this boy whom God heard?
2. What is the meaning of this boy's name? See Genesis 16:11.
3. Do you think this boy knew God? Do you think his father taught him about the God who made heaven and earth?
4. Do you think this boy believed in the promise from Genesis 3:15?

Theology
Some of the questions raised in this section do not have clear answers from Scripture. Every indication is that Ishmael was taught by his father all about the promises of God and the works of God. It likely was not pleasant to learn that he was not the promised child, that another (his half-brother Isaac) was instead. Yet Ishmael was circumcised along with Abram, he received protection from God, blessing from God (see Genesis 16 and 21:18), and God gave him 13 years alone with his father Abram. The story of Ishmael is one of conflict, but it is also one of God listening to his children, wherever they are.

3

Genesis 26:24 "Fear not, for I am with you and will bless you."

Read first: Genesis 26:23-25

This instance of "Fear not!" is the briefest in all the Bible. We are not given any reasons why God comes to Isaac or what Isaac may have been feeling prior to the moment. The text does not say Isaac is in any mortal danger and God does not reveal anything which might make him tremble. We do also know that this isn't the first time and it will not be the last time God speaks to Isaac.

This is, importantly, the first time we hear what will be a common refrain, "I am with you." The presence of God will be the main reason from now on that a person is to not fear. We will not always be specifically told what benefit God's presence is, just that it is or it will be. Of course parents naturally say and do the same for their children. If a child is scared because of a nightmare we reassure them that everything will be alright and we are there with them. When they face a trial or a new challenge we often encourage them by going along.

There is something special in the presence of one whom we believe can vanquish the evils around us, something special in the presence of a parent or loved one – even if we know we must still perform on our own.

How much more special, more meaningful, is the presence of the Almighty Father?!

Prayer: Ask your heavenly Father to comfort you and hold you close.

> "Where, then, is evil, and whence, and how crept it in hither? What is its root, and what its seed? Or hath it no being at all? Why, then, do we fear and shun that which hath no being? Or if we fear it needlessly, then surely: is that fear evil whereby the heart is unnecessarily pricked and tormented,-and so much a greater evil, as we have naught to fear, and yet do fear. Therefore either that is evil which we fear, or the act of fearing is in itself evil. Whence, therefore, is it, seeing that God, who is good, hath made all these things good? He, indeed, the greatest and chiefest Good, hath created these lesser goods; but both Creator and created are all good."
> – Augustine, Confessions, Book VII

Diving In

"This is, importantly, the first time we hear what will be a common refrain, 'I am with you.' The presence of God will be the main reason from now on that a person is to not fear. We will not always be specifically told what benefit God's presence is, just that it is or it will be."

Question
1. Is God with you?
2. Which Bible passages teach you the answer to #1?
3. What proof do you have that an invisible God, a God who is spirit, is with you?

Theology

The presence of God is a rich Biblical teaching. From God being present at creation, present in the Garden, present on Mt. Sinai, present in the tabernacle and the temple, present in his son Immanuel, present in the Supper of Christ, to God being present in Jesus always, "even to the end of the age", the presence of God is constant, everywhere, and is the reward and blessing of God's faithful children.

Perhaps it is because God is not visible that he reminds us continually that he is present. After all, we tend to gauge reality by what we see, feel, hear, and experience. Yet, as we know, there are many things which we cannot see, or feel, or hear, or directly experience, that are nonetheless real. Take for example the light which bounced off this text to the other side of the room. Just because your eyes were not over there to receive that light, does not make that light any less real.

The teaching of the Christian church is that God is present in his word, in the sacraments which carry his promise, and in the

Holy Spirit which lives in believers in Christ. God is also evident in creation, and creation testifies to God's presence. See Romans 1 and 2 and Psalm 19.

Question

1. Perhaps the most relevant consideration, however, is what God's presence does for you. What does it matter that God is with you? Consider the parable in Mark 3 about the strong man, or God's promises in Isaiah 49:24-26.
2. Is God's presence more than strength and protection? Consider John 14:16 and 26, 15:26 and 16:7-11.
3. Consider Matthew 18:20.
4. How would you pray for God's presence in your life – as a presence of protection, conviction, teaching?

4

Genesis 46:3 "Fear not to go down to Egypt, for there I will make you into a great nation."

Read first: Genesis 46:1-4

In order to understand God's word to Jacob it is best to put ourselves in Jacob's sandals. Who is Jacob, and what might he be experiencing, that God would feel it necessary to speak to him?

First, we know that Jacob was an older man; he would live in Goshen seventeen years before he died at the age of 147. His favorite wife Rachel, for whom Jacob had worked fourteen years, was dead and her firstborn son, as far as Jacob knew had died at the mouth and claws of some vicious beast. There was also a years-long famine happening in the land and when his sons had gone to Egypt the first time, one of them had gotten into some trouble and had been imprisoned.

But then comes news of Joseph, the favored son, being reborn – as it were. Suddenly he is alive, a powerful ruler in the most powerful nation on earth. How did that come to be, Jacob no doubt wondered. And what would his boy do with all this power once he had his family living nearby? Would he feel angry at them for not searching out and finding their lost brother and son? Would Joseph be resentful towards his father for all the lost years? Would

Joseph even care? Most importantly for Jacob, would Joseph love his father? How could he – abandoned, lost, alone, unloved, scared for so many long days and nights, helpless for so many years?

Now we begin to sympathize with Jacob and we can begin to imagine Jacob's fears, emotions, concerns. Any father with heart and soul would fear – not the journey to Egypt – the journey back into relationship with his lost and now found favorite son. Therefore, God's words to Jacob are ones of love and compassion spoken from one Father to another father. God knew that Joseph still loved his father and he knew Jacob needed a word of peace and comfort. Even more, God's words reveal special love, "Joseph's hand shall close your eyes." Jacob could rest assured that Joseph would love his father to the end of his earthly days; Joseph would be there at the end to receive his blessing. They would be side by side; neither lost nor hurting, both comforting one another. And of course we hear God's promise of his presence; that we should not fear because, "I myself will go down with you."

Prayer: Ask your Father in heaven first for forgiveness and second that He would reveal His presence to you.

Diving In

Theology

    The story of Jacob and Joseph is one of the longest in the Bible. From Genesis 25 to Genesis 40 we read the saga of a family struggling from the womb for dominance, identity, survival, and love. This epic is well worth reading again and again if not for its drama then certainly for its lessons and insights.

Question

1. The fear that Jacob felt was an unspoken one. But it was not unknown to God. What unspoken fears might your Father in heaven be well aware of?
2. Some fears we never experience; some because we do not live long enough, some because events do not happen to bring such fears to reality. What are some fears that your family or loved ones feel which you personally do not experience?

"But then comes news of Joseph, the favored son, being reborn – as it were. Suddenly he is alive, a powerful ruler in the most powerful nation on earth."

Question

1. When you see your children, your siblings, your believing family in heaven, what might you feel?
2. Are you looking forward to your reunions in heaven or only mourning their absence here on earth?

Theology

The Bible assumes that we will recognize those who have gone before us into heaven. We should rejoice in this teaching and knowledge and live our earthly life in anticipation of such joy that we cannot presently imagine. Consider, on this teaching, Genesis 25:8 and Numbers 27:12 where God indicates that there is life and identification beyond this earthly existence. David in 2 Samuel 12:23 makes a similar statement. Peter in Luke 9:33 demonstrates that we can even know those whom we have not seen. See also Matthew 8:11. Paul makes some very encouraging statements in Ephesians 3:15 and 1 Corinthians 13:12.

"Even more, God's words reveal special love, 'Joseph's hand shall close your eyes.' Jacob could rest assured that Joseph would love his father to the end of his earthly days; Joseph would be there at the end to receive his blessing. They would be side by side; neither lost nor hurting, both comforting one another."

Question

1. Where is your family? Specifically, are you living far from your parents, grandparents, children, grand children?
2. What steps did Joseph take to reunite his family?
3. Did Joseph really need to bring his family to Egypt? Couldn't he just have sent regular shipments of food, clothing, and wealth? Couldn't the extended family just have come for a vacation?
4. Are fears more easily handled when someone is alone or when someone is in a strong and supportive family?
5. How important in the Bible is family, the idea of family, the practice of family, the establishment of family? (You will find that there are few things more important than

family in the Bible. So, exactly what are you doing to create, maintain and protect your family?)

Theology

Here are some verses about family. Read each one and begin to construct a theology, a Biblical teaching, on the family.

1. Genesis 1:28 _____

2. 1 Timothy 5:8 _____

3. Ephesians 6:1-4 _____

4. Matthew 19:1-15 _____

5. Leviticus 19:17-18 _____

6. Proverbs 18:22 _____

7. Ephesians 5 _____

8. Psalm 127 _____

9. Psalm 128 _____

10. Proverbs 17:6 _____

11. Proverbs 13:22 _____

12. Psalm 145:4 _____

13. Joshua 24:15 _____

14. Genesis 18:19 _____

15. Proverbs 31 _____

16. Proverbs 15:20 _____

17. Ruth _____

18. 1 Timothy 3 _____

19. 2 Timothy 1:5 _____

20. Psalm 103:17 _____

5

Numbers 21:34 "Fear not him, for I have given him into your hand, and all his people, and his land."

Read first: Numbers 21:31-35

This instance of "Fear not!", like the one in Genesis 15 with Abram, does not initially make sense in light of the prior chapters and the context of Moses' life. For all of chapter 21, Moses and the Israelites have been dominating: they defeated Arad in verse 3, Sihon in verse 21. They had also been provided for: God gave them healing in verse 9 and water in verse 16. Israel was having such positive times they made up two songs along the way to sing in celebration. Now comes the king of Bashan, named Og, and God comes to strengthen and reassure Moses. Remember, this is the man who witnessed the plagues, the parted sea, the dead Egyptian army, and who walked up and down the mountain to meet God. What could possibly give this man fear, or reason to want to be afraid?

To understand what Moses saw when he beheld the king of Bashan, we need to refer to a number of Bible passages which lead us to the knowledge that Og was a stunningly large human being. Moses will recount the story in Deuteronomy 3 and say, "For only Og the king of Bashan was left of the remnant of the Rephaim." This word 'Rephaim' is also translated in other places by the

English word 'giants'. Then Moses goes on and says, "Behold, his bed is nine cubits in length, and four cubits in breadth." That makes the bed a whopping 13 feet long and 6 feet wide. This means that Og probably stood upwards of a stunning 11 to 12 feet in height.

Now we can imagine the sight that Moses and Israel experienced as they went out to battle. Fear? Yes, probably. Anytime something massive bears down on us with intent to kill we naturally feel a bit of apprehension. But God didn't want Israel, or Moses, to turn and run. So He came. He spoke the words. "Fear not!" Why not? "For I have given him into your hand."

I love the past tense that God uses so often regarding our battles and struggles and sins. "Fear not, it's already over, done, taken care of. Simply behold the majesty and power of the almighty God!"

Prayer: Praise your Father in heaven for making your sins 'past tense' events and for blessing you with a future filled with His joy and love.

> "One thing alone I charge you, considering it a necessity, that having the fear of the Lord before your eyes you will put Him first, and carry on all things with your wanted concord as men of wisdom and understanding."
> – Athanasius, Letter XLVII. To the Church of Alexandria on the Same Occasion.

Diving In

Question

1. Was Moses ever afraid? Read Exodus 2:14 and 3:6.

"To understand what Moses saw when he beheld the king of Bashan, we need to refer to a number of Bible passages which lead us to the knowledge that Og was a stunningly large human being."

Question
1. Was Og really a giant?
2. After reading the teaching information below, consider these Bible passages: Deuteronomy 2:8-11, Numbers 13:25-33, Genesis 6:4, and Amos 2:9-10.

Theology

To understand what Moses saw when he beheld the king of Bashan, we need to turn to Deuteronomy 3 where Moses is in the beginning of his book-long historical review and theological summation. He recounts Numbers 21 in Deuteronomy 3:1-11 and provides a helpful set of facts to those who were not alive to see Og in all his glory.

Moses says in verse 11, "For only Og the king of Bashan was left of the remnant of the Rephaim." This word 'Rephaim' is also translated in other places by the English word 'giants' – which paints an intriguing picture of Moses and Israel going to war against giants. But Moses tells us more in verse 11, "Behold, his bed was a bed of iron. Is it not in Rabbah of the Ammonites? Nine cubits was its length, and four cubits its breadth, according to the common cubit." Presuming that a 'common cubit' is close to 18 inches, that makes the iron bed a whopping 13 feet long and 6 feet wide. Taking off a foot for the space an individual needs for a pillow, and assuming Og didn't like to have his feet near the edge, we can figure that Og may have stood upwards of a stunning 11 to 12 feet in height.

As astounding as this may be, and as preposterous as it may seem looking at human stature today, Moses provides two pieces of additional corroboration to quell any doubts. First, he calls the people to recall the bed – and, if they have any doubts about Moses' measurements, they can make their own observations at the "Og Museum of Natural History" in Rabbah. Second, the bed is made of iron. This is remarkable – how much weight could that bed hold? Surely the weight of a 12 foot giant!

6

Joshua 1:9 "Fear not, and do not be dismayed, for the Lord your God is with you wherever you go."

Read first: Joshua 1:1-9

This word from God comes at the end of a speech / lecture / command / injunction / exhortation (yes, it is really all of those) which the Lord gives to Joshua "after the death of Moses my servant" and prior to the entrance of Israel into the Promised Land. This section of the word of God may be divided into two parts of 10. In one part we have 10 commands or exhortations made by God to Joshua. In the second part we have 10 statements of what God has, is, and is going to do.

When we look at this communication by God as a whole, it seems as though God is really preparing Joshua for some wild times ahead. Consider what a parent says when sending their child out driving for the first time. "Watch out for the other cars!" "Watch out for people, animals too!" "Be careful." "Be safe!" "Know the rules, laws, customs." "Expect the unexpected." "Keep an eye on the gas tank gauge." And so on and so forth. God tells Joshua to be strong, careful, courageous, to go and do, to meditate, and to not depart from the Law. He is trying to prepare him for what is to come in the days ahead.

God is a father who is heavily involved and invested in his children and in the earthly leader he has chosen. He wants Joshua to lead God's people in battle and in Godly example. Yet God knows what lies ahead – the enemies, the perils, the temptations, and he knows the weaknesses of his people; their great tendency to sin and forgo an intimate relationship with their Father God. And, since God loves his people so much, he seeks to care and to provide for them.

He doesn't want them to sit back and relax, however. He wants them, he even expects them, to be engaged. Their journey, and ours, is not a journey for the faint-hearted. The path that God sets us on is a path of challenge, struggle, victory and prize. Big, ugly, terror-inducing people and events lie ahead but we can be sure every one of them is but a passing irritation to the God who goes with us.

Prayer: Talk with your Father in heaven about courage, about engagement, about how He is preparing you for His work.

> "So long then as by a lamp we walk, it is needful that with fear we should live."
> – Augustine, Expositions on the Psalms: Psalm 52

Diving In

Theology

Just a note: the second phrase in Joshua 1:9, "do not be dismayed", is variously translated as terror, panic, shattered, broken and may be thus read as a synonym which intensifies the Lord's word to Joshua, "Fear not!"

"This section of the word of God may be divided into two parts of 10. In one part we have 10 commands or exhortations made by God to Joshua. In the second part we have 10 statements of what God has, is, and is going to do. . . . He doesn't want them to sit back and relax, however. He wants them, he even expects them, to be engaged."

Question

1. Which of God's commands to Joshua suggest he should, or God's people should, sit back and relax?
2. What might this teach us about our life of faith?

Theology

The chart here shows a pattern in the first chapter of Joshua. Notice the balance God achieves between what he wants and expects and what he has done and promised. There is also a balance, which you may discover on your own, between what God has done and what God will do, and between what Joshua is to do and what he is to make a habit of.

Commands / Exhortations	God: has, is, will do
Go over the Jordan	I am giving them land
Be strong and courageous	I have given you where you tread
Be strong and very courageous	I promised Moses
Do not turn left or right	No man shall stand before you
Law shall not depart from your mouth	I was with Moses
Meditate on the Book day and night	I will be with you
Be careful to do all that is written	I will not leave you / forsake you
Make way prosperous / good success	I swore to their fathers
Be strong and courageous	I commanded you
Do not be frightened or dismayed	I am with you

Theology

The number 10 is found in some fairly interesting places in the Bible. Beyond the 10 Commandments, the 10 plagues, the 10 sons of Leah, the 10 steps of Hezekiah, the 10 sons of Haman, as well as the 10 cleansed lepers and the 10 virgins and the 10 talents of Jesus parables, we are told that Noah was the 10th generation from Adam and Abram was the 10th generation from Shem, the son of Noah.

Without being able to be completely certain, the 10 names / generations from Adam to Noah hold a potentially significant set of meanings. While the names of people in the Bible were almost always burgeoning with meaning, we can only make an educated guess on names to which we are not given specific information. Still, the 10 names* offer this possible dramatic sentence:

> Man is appointed mortality and sorrow. The Blessed God shall come with teaching and his death shall bring the poor comfort.

	Name	Meaning
1	Adam	Man
2	Seth	appointed
3	Enos	mortal / sick
4	Cainan	to get sorrow
5	Mahalaleel	praise/bless God
6	Jared	shall come down
7	Enoch	teaching / discipline
8	Methuselah	his death shall bring / send
9	Lamech	the sorrowful / poor / low
10	Noah	comfort / consolation

*Sources: Hitchcock's Bible Names Dictionary and Brown-Driver-Briggs Enhanced Hebrew/English Lexicon.

7

Joshua 8:1 "Fear not and do not be dismayed."

Read first: Joshua 7:1-9, 8:1-3

While these words to Joshua are a repetition of what God said to him when Israel entered Canaan, the circumstances now are quite different. Joshua and Israel are dismayed, confused and probably a bit uneasy. After the total defeat and destruction of Jericho, a most massive city, the now mighty Israelite nation falls in battle to tiny Ai. They have unexpectedly received their first 'bloody nose' in Canaan, losing 1% of their fighting force in a losing battle which should have been a lopsided victory.

After crying out to God, who not-so-gently rebukes Joshua for his passionate outburst at God, the Israelites purge the sin (and the sinner) from their nation. Then God comes to Joshua and tells him, "Fear not!" because Ai has – past tense again – been given in victory to Israel.

This is a reassuring word, not simply for those facing battle, but in knowing God's holy people have followed God's holy will and He moves forward now with them. Sometimes we get carried away with these experiences, fooling ourselves into thinking that our repentance earned God's favorable attitude towards our next course of action. The fact is that while repentance is the necessary part and life of a Christian, it does not automatically make our next choices God-pleasing. After repentance, and before we step foot on our chosen path, we must submit that path to God for his approval and blessing.

Israel very clearly knew what their path was because God had told them that Ai was next on the checklist of cities to conquer. Still, there is a bit of humor in Israel's next action after hearing that the defeat of Ai is secure. They bring to the battle ten times as many forces as previously sent; 30,000 instead of 3,000. Indeed they trust God, but they also try to leave nothing to chance!

Prayer: Talk to God the Father about how your defeats were actually God teaching you and revealing Himself to you.

> And what are fear and sadness but a volition of aversion from the things which we do not wish? But when consent takes the form of seeking to possess the things we wish, this is called desire; and when consent takes the form of enjoying the things we wish, this is called joy. In like manner, when we turn with aversion from that which we do not wish to happen, this volition is termed fear; and when we turn away from that which has happened against our will, this act of will is called sorrow.
>
> – Augustine, City of God, Book XIV

Diving In

Read, at a minimum, Joshua 7:1-9, 8:1-3

"After crying out to God, who not-so-gently rebukes Joshua for his passionate outburst at God, the Israelites purge the sin (and the sinner) from their nation."

Question
1. Consider Joshua 7:7. This is a common question God hears: "God, why did you do this to me?" Why do we often think our troubles come as a direct result of God's dislike, distrust or discontent with us? How would you respond if, after telling your child to not touch the flame, they did and then turned to you and asked, "Why did you do this to me?"
2. Consider Joshua 7:11. God answers the "Why?" question with, "You brought this on yourself." In other words, God did not initiate this trouble, the people did. What (erroneous) assumptions did the people make? Do we make the same assumptions?
3. Is it easier to blame God for our troubles or to see the fault in ourselves?
4. Why does God tell Joshua to "Get up!" (twice)? Does God not want Joshua's prayer?

"After repentance, and before we step foot on our chosen path, we must submit that path to God for his approval and blessing."

Question

1. We all fall different places on the continuum of prayer. Do you offer to God all decisions / steps? Do you offer God the major decisions and occasional steps along the path? Do you offer to God the major decisions once they haven't worked out the way you hoped?

Theology

Proverbs holds the greatest wisdom for decision making. "In all your ways acknowledge the Lord, and he will make straight your paths." "Ponder the path of your feet, then all your ways will be sure." "The heart of man plans his way, but the Lord establishes his steps." When it comes to decisions, the Christian uses the head, heart, and knees and the Lord moves the feet where he wills. What is confusing sometimes is when our feet take us a direction we did not plan. God's answer to our prayers may not be a loud "No." or even a gentle rebuke. He may simply guide us in a different direction as a parent does to a toddler learning to walk. Are you ready and willing to be on a different path? Whatever the path, we know it will be a path of righteousness and victory in His name.

8

Joshua 10:8 "Fear not them, for I have given them into your hands."

Read first: Joshua 10:1-11

Before Joshua set foot in the Promised Land, God told him not to be frightened. Before the second battle at Ai, God tells Joshua not to fear. And now, with his third battle set before him, God comes again and tells Joshua to not fear because the predetermined outcome rests in his favor.

Jericho was a single city and so too Ai. But chapter 10 introduces us to an alliance of nations, or kings, joined to fight a common enemy, namely Israel. This escalation of the hostilities may have caused panic among the troops – or it may not have. Perhaps God was preempting the awakening of human fear. Regardless, the victory was amazing because Israel clearly saw that while their might and numbers may have been impressive, it was the God of Israel who was fighting – and winning – the battle.

Does God need Joshua and Israel in order to win the battle? No, but he does need them to be witnesses. And as if to make them feel involved, he lets them do a bit of janitorial work – enough to 'keep it real'; enough to form a narrative that is passed down from father to son. These narratives are greatly important in communicating the saving acts of God to the next generation. In the case of Israel, the narrative may have begun something like this: "Let me tell you, my son, about your grandad and why there are stones in front of the cave at Makkedah."

What is your story of God's victory over evil? How does your narrative about the work of God in your family and in your life begin? What can you say about the part you played in God's battle? What will your children hear about the God who said (to you?), "Fear not!"

Prayer: Ask your heavenly Father for the words and wisdom necessary to tell the right stories.

> "For if without the aid of fear temporal things can never be achieved, how much less spiritual matters; for I desire to know, who ever learnt his letters without fear? who has become a proficient in any art, without fear?"
> – John Chrysostom, Homilies on Philippians, VIII, ca. 400A.D.

Diving In

"In the case of Israel, the narrative may have begun something like this: 'Let me tell you, my son, about your grandad and why there are stones in front of the cave at Makkedah.'"

Question

1. What stories do you tell your children? What tales of heroes and battles, defeats and victories, maidens and rescues fill the minds and hearts of the young people in your home? Are they all what modern man has conceived or are they the true events of God's work in history?

Theology

The greatest story passed down in ancient Israel was the story of the Passover. God specifically set up the narrative, the question and answer process, and the expectations.

Exodus 13:13-15 "Every firstborn of a donkey you shall redeem with a lamb, or if you will not redeem it you shall break its neck. Every firstborn of man among your sons you shall redeem. And when in time to come your son asks you, 'What does this mean?' you shall say to him, 'By a strong hand the LORD brought us out of Egypt, from the house of slavery. For when Pharaoh stubbornly refused to let us go, the LORD killed all the firstborn in the land of Egypt, both the firstborn of man and the firstborn of animals.'"

Moses followed this pattern in Deuteronomy 6:20 when the son asked about the Law and Joshua also created a question and answer narrative about the 12 stones in Joshua 4. Most of the rest of the historical books in the Old Testament, along with Psalms, the Gospels, and Acts are packed full of great battles, struggles, victories and lessons. Each and every part of the Bible was written for our instruction.

Making good use of these narratives is a skill that separates the average man from the man who is listened to, respected, and honored in his home and church. To have this skill a man must first know the Bible. He must know the stories, the characters, the sequence of events. And more than knowing, he must be able to tell these stories with passion. This man of wisdom also knows the lessons and the key elements from each story. He knows if a story is about a young man or woman or if it is a story for parents. He knows if a story teaches patience, creativeness, purity, or attentiveness. Finally, this great man watches his family and his community for connections and similarities between the life now and the life of God's past people and he produces with love and in the proper time, a story and a lesson from God's word.

Everyone loves a good story and there is none greater than the Gospel. How about telling a good story today?

9

Joshua 11:6 "Fear not in the face of them, for tomorrow at this time I will give over all of them, slain, to Israel."

Read first: Joshua 11:1-9

Three battles, three exact phrasings of "Fear Not!" A coincidence? Probably not. Ai, the alliance of Adonizedek and now the alliance of Jabin which was so massive it is described as a "great horde in number like the sand that is on the sea shore." This superlative description is likely not a precise counting of the number of soldiers on the plain, but it clearly tells that the armed forces facing Israel were frighteningly overwhelming.

Yet, God is there, reassuring, predicting victory, telling Joshua what God will do and what Joshua will end up doing. The number of foes does not matter to God; notice God never numbers his enemies. Victory is what God sees and a total lack of fear at the forces of men and evil is what God communicates to His chosen children.

Fear not? It is pretty easy to walk this path when the walls of Jericho fall without an Israelite hand touching them, when God directs the attack on Ai through Joshua's javelin and when hail falls so hard it kills fleeing soldiers. Do we have these mighty signs and actions from God today? I think few would say we do.

Maybe we don't have these, or don't see them, for one singular reason. Are we even on a path that travels to God's enemies? Perhaps we fear not, and see not, because we are still wandering around in the wilderness avoiding conflict with those who set themselves up against God. Perhaps we do not see God's actions, or God in action, because we have not taken up the armor of God and entered the battle.

God could tell Joshua and Israel to "Fear not!" because they were facing, no – attacking!, scary people. Perhaps to hear the words of God we want to hear we need to be where God is working and winning.

Prayer: Pray that your Father would prepare you for battle, but if this is not His will, pray He would prepare you to minister to those who do.

> "On this account, even though innumerable wolves encompass thee, and many crowds of wicked doers, I fear nothing; but I pray both that existing temptations may be suppressed, and that others may not occur, thus fulfilling the Lord's precept who bids us pray that we may not enter into temptation; but if it should be permitted to happen again I have good confidence concerning thy golden soul, which acquires therefrom the greatest riches for itself."
> – John Chrysostom, Letter To Olympias, IV

Diving In

"Are we even on a path that travels to God's enemies? Perhaps we fear not, and see not, because we are still wandering around in the wilderness avoiding conflict with those who set themselves up against God. Perhaps we do not see God's actions, or God in action, because we have not taken up the armor of God and entered the battle."

Theology

The difference between a disciple and an apostle is purpose. A disciple's purpose is to stay and learn. An apostle's purpose is to go where they are sent and do what they have been asked. Luke 6:13 has one of the most clear statements on the difference: "And when day came, Jesus called his disciples and chose from them twelve, whom he named apostles: Simon, whom he named Peter, and Andrew his brother. . ." Mark 3:14 is also helpful: "And Jesus appointed twelve, whom he also named apostles, so that they might be with him and he might send them out to preach and have authority to cast out demons."

There are times in our life when we are disciples and times when we are sent by the Lord. Like the disciples, we may have a mission and then return for more learning. Like the disciples, we cannot always stay at home in the comfort of a safe learning environment. Not only does the Lord wish us to go and do, some lessons are best learned 'in the field' rather than 'in the classroom'.

Question

1. Where are God's enemies in your vicinity? Where is Satan attacking your family? Where is your church in spiritual conflict? How is your community coming under pressure from ungodly ideas, practices or people?

2. Armor is useless to protect you if you do not wear it. Consider the armor of God (Ephesians 6). What is each piece of armor used to protect you against?

3. Armor can be dangerous to the wearer if it is not used correctly. Improperly worn armor can be a hindrance to safety. What pieces of the armor of God are you trained to put on and use? Which do you feel you would like more training with?

4. Soldiers go out to battle. Where is God calling you to enter the battle? You may not be on the front lines, but there are many aspects to a confrontation. What skills and gifts has God given you to help his front-line soldiers?

10

Judges 6:23 "Peace be to you. Fear not; you shall not die."

Read first: Judges 6:11-24

Honestly, Gideon was a complainer, a whiner, easily compromised, a coward, and in the end nothing but a whoring charlatan. Still, God chose him for service. And God has mercifully chosen us, who are just as sinful, to serve Him in all our varied capacities. And that is really what this "Fear Not" is all about – mercy.

To get a sense of what Gideon felt we need to understand what he knew about seeing God face to face. Gideon apparently knew his history pretty well, because he knew he should die if he saw God. Previous encounters with God did go pretty well for the human, though, if not for each one having a bit of scariness involved. Abraham met the angels who soon after destroyed Sodom and Gomorrah. Jacob wrestled with God and that resulted in a dislocated hip. Moses met with God and even tried to see him face to face and these encounters resulted in everyone being afraid of Moses because he glowed afterwards. Israel met with God at Mount Sinai and they all felt like they were going to die – but they survived.

Also, to get a sense of what Gideon felt, we need to experience our smallness in the face of God's true awesomeness. But words cannot convey very well the smallness one feels when in the presence of overwhelming power. You may have been near a tornado, too close to wildfires, or felt earthquakes but have you ever felt the power of an erupting volcano, a hurricane, or a tsunami wave? We can feel very small in the face of the power of disturbed nature; but how much smaller would we feel in the presence of All Mighty, All Powerful, All Knowing, All Present, All Existing God? Would not our mighty sins glare with such intensity that we should feel like dying? Yes. Most certainly!

And the Word of God comes to the cowering, sinful, despairing man to tell him, and to tell us, "Fear not!" "Shalom to you!" You shall not die. Like the men before you, God is merciful to you. Is God to be feared? Amazingly, the answer is both yes and no. God's holy and perfect nature stands against and must destroy sin. And He would also destroy the sinner were God not also the peace-giver and the forgiver of all sins. Here we meet God's Justice and God's Mercy – all in one true God. His justice we are right to be afraid of and his mercy we are right to fear with all reverence.

Prayer: Talk with your Father in heaven about faith that surpasses all attempts of the human flesh to destroy it.

Diving In

"Here we meet God's Justice and God's Mercy – all in one true God. His justice we are right to be afraid of and his mercy we are right to fear with all reverence."

Question

1. Having sinned, what is your just punishment? In case you don't already know, read what God says about those who sin – even just once: Genesis 2:16-17, Psalm 14, Proverbs 6:16-19, Luke 12:5, Romans 3:9-20, 6:23, Hebrews 10:30-31. (There are many, many more passages we could read on the justice and punishment God promises to sinners and violators of His law.)

2. Having believed in Jesus for salvation, what is your just reward? In case you don't already know, read what God says about those who are in Christ: Genesis 3:15, Exodus 15:13, Isaiah 53, Luke 24:46-47, John 1:36, Romans 6:23, Hebrews 8:8-12. (There are many, many more passages we could read on the mercy and forgiveness God promises to believers in His son.)

Theology

The justice and the mercy of God sometimes appear to be at opposite poles. Often it has been asked how a merciful God can be a God who punishes humans with a promised everlasting torment. Alternatively it may be questioned why God, who is just, holy, perfect and righteous needs to have any sort of compassion, mercy or grace upon a broken, inherently and continually rebellious, creation.

The reality that God is both merciful and just at the same time, as he describes himself in his word, is similar to the reality that God is one and yet three. (One essence and at the same time three persons.) No amount of discussion or reasoning will take us to a place of comprehension on the nature of God. What we can see, with insight from church fathers before us, is that God has provided a way, a means, for us to survive his justice and yet he, at the same time, has provided a way, a means, for his justice to be fulfilled.

The way, the means, of which we speak is Jesus Christ. Taking upon the sin of the world, he suffered the just punishment for such sins. Having died for sin, Jesus satisfies the demands of God's justice. God then raises Christ from the dead and announces that all who believe in his son will escape what they deserve and they will instead be given life. This free pass, as it were, from death to life, was anything but free. Jesus paid for the pass with his life. How incredible it is that faith receives the pass for free!

11

1 Kings 17:13 "Fear not, go and do as you have said."

Read first: 1 Kings 17:1-16

This "Fear not!" is a promise of an ongoing miracle and a test of trust in the God of Israel (not of Sidon; see Luke 4:26). Elijah has left Israel in a severe drought and traveled, under the direction of God, outside the country to the home of a widow. She and her son are one meal away from starvation. Elijah speaks a ridiculous demand of her: "Feed me first." But he does follow that request with a promise. Now the promise is a bit vague – who knows when it will rain in Israel? Tomorrow? Next week? Next year?

Unfortunately, God does not always give us the details we might like. The reason for this may be that if he did we'd have so many other questions that we wouldn't get around to doing what he asked of us in the first place. So too this widow. Her task was to discover that the God of Israel was real, and really powerful outside of Israel – the rest of the details would come later.

Faith outside of Israel is a theme in the Bible and this faith seems to come easily, more easily in fact, than it does to those inside Israel. Is it easier to trust in God if you haven't been raised 'in the faith'? Perhaps faith is more child-like in these situations. After all, what did the widow have to lose? Trust a foreign God with a great promise and risk losing a tiny meal that really wouldn't do her a whole lot of good or dismiss the foreign God and keep the worthless crumbs? The message to "Fear not!" surely does not know geographic or cultural bounds so the widow seems to have heard it with all the hope and trust it was intended to create.

This is a not-so-subtle message that none of God's creatures are meant to live in fear. Rather, they should seek and find the One who can grant fearless living. This is a message as well for the household of faith. We should not keep such good news to ourselves but seek other people with whom we can share this God-given news and lifestyle.

Prayer: Ask your Father in heaven to show you a person outside the faith to whom you should share the fantastic news of salvation in Jesus.

"Was there any disciple who could be free from fear, after Peter, who was the most confident and forward of them all, was told, 'The cock shall not crow till thou hast denied me thrice'? Considering themselves, therefore, beginning with Peter, as destined to perish, they all had cause to be troubled: but when they now hear, 'In my Father's house are many mansions: if it were not so, I would have told you; for I go to prepare a place for you,' they are revived from their trouble, made certain and confident that after all the perils of temptations they shall dwell with Christ in the presence of God."
– Augustine, Tractates on John, LXVII

Diving In

"Faith outside of Israel is a theme in the Bible and this faith seems to come easily, more easily in fact than it does to those inside Israel."

Question

1. Make a list of individuals who were outside of Israel, yet had faith in the God of Israel. What did they have in common? Why are they included in the Bible – what purpose do their stories hold for us today? Here are some Bible references to get you started: Joshua 2, Ruth 1, Jonah 3, Mark 7, Acts 10.

Theology

The teaching here holds the themes that (1) God is the God of all people, the whole world, not only believers, that (2) Israel was chosen *not to hold exclusive rights* to God's word and Name but they were chosen *to demonstrate life* under the Name of God and (3) that we are expected to see all people as people for whom Christ died and as potential believers in Christ.

Sometimes it is said that there is no mission, or mission emphasis, in the Old Testament. In fact, there is great mission emphasis in the whole Bible; though it is expressed differently in the Old than in the New Testament. In the Old Testament we see God's people as possessors of His Word and His Name, but not as hidden treasures, rather as revealed treasures awaiting the finding and participation of the nations (Deuteronomy 4:5-8). In the New Testament God's people possess the revealed plan of God's salvation through his son (Hebrews 2:1-4). Again, this is not a hidden treasure, and this time it is a message to be delivered to all the world. In the New Testament age, God's people not only demonstrate life under the Name of God, they go out and proclaim the grace and forgiveness found in God's Name. In both the Old and New Testament worlds, all the peoples on the planet observe God's people living in God's kingdom. The greater mission in the New Testament age is the commission to go and tell the Good News.

For theme (1) look at these passages and note how God makes universal claim:

1. Exodus 19:5 _____

2. Deuteronomy 10:14 _____

3. Psalm 24:1 _____

4. Jonah 4:11 _____

5. Acts 10:34 _____

6. Romans 1:18-2:11 _____

For theme (2) look at these passages and note God's expectations of his people:

1. Genesis 12:3 _____

2. Deuteronomy 4:6-8 _____

3. Joshua 4:19-24 _____

4. 1 Kings 8:41-43 _____

5. Galatians 3:8 _____

6. 1 Peter 2:9 _____

For theme (3) look at these passages and note God's expectation of salvation:

1. Psalm 22:27 _____

2. Isaiah 49:6 _____

3. Luke 2:29-32 _____

4. Luke 24:44-48 _____

5. John 8:12 _____

6. Acts 10:34-35 _____

12

2 Kings 1:15 "Go down with him; fear not him."

Read first: 2 Kings 1:2-17

In the second book of the Kings in Scripture, we are well into the time of the split kingdom of Israel. Jehoshaphat is king in Judah and Ahaziah is king in Israel (the part of the whole nation which kept the name after the separation). Elijah is God's prophet at this time and he has previously faced off with King Ahab, Queen Jezebel, and God, in a sense, at Horeb. Elijah has been on the run most of his life but now he sits on a hill. A hill with one hundred and two charred corpses lying around – all made so by Elijah's command. It must have been quite the scene!

A third military captain with his fifty armed men shows up. He's not so haughty as the previous captains. He falls to his knees, begs for his life. And an angel of God tells Elijah to "Fear Not!" . . . Okay, this is confusing. What is Elijah supposed to be afraid of? He can call down fire on his enemies. He's faced the bad guys repeatedly and won. God and Elijah got things worked out on Mt. Horeb. He's even got a replacement prophet in the wings and God has promised that He will take care of the remaining bad guys through Hazel, Jehu and Elisha. Can Elijah really be afraid of little-old Ahaziah who is dying on his bed? Can he really be afraid of this captain on his knees?

Oh the mysteries of Scripture! We are not told what Elijah is afraid of, or what he should not be afraid of – we can only speculate. One reasonable thought is that Elijah fears bodily harm. It is in his nature, sinful and human, to fear pain, or torture, or physical distress. In light of how God has in the past provided Elijah with protection and sustenance this thought has some merit. The fact is that some men do not fear bodily harm as other men do. Some men can speak before thousands while other men wilt at the thought. Prick that seemingly courageous man and he will crumble while the man who cowers at crowds will tell you to put some effort behind your next poke.

God knows our weaknesses and he leads us not into temptation but he delivers us from evil. God knows our fears. Do we think God would really place us in situations where we would succumb to our fears? Or do we trust that God will guard and protect us from/in our sinfulness so that his will would be accomplished?

Prayer: Talk with your Father in heaven about the necessary trust
you need to have in Him.

Diving In

"Elijah has been on the run most of his life but now he sits on a hill. A hill with a hundred and two charred corpses lying around – all made so by Elijah's command. It must have been quite the scene!"

Question

1. Calling down fire from heaven seems to be Elijah's modus operandi. Consider these other connections between Elijah and fire:
    1. 1 Kings 18
    2. 1 Kings 19
    3. 2 Kings 1 (this lesson)
    4. 2 Kings 2
    5. Luke 1:17 with 3:9 and 3:17 (Admittedly not a very close connection, but nonetheless interesting!)

"God knows our weaknesses and he leads us not into temptation but he delivers us from evil. God knows our fears. Do we think God would really place us in situations where we would succumb to our fears? Or do we trust that God will guard and protect us from/in our sinfulness so that his will would be accomplished?"

Theology

There is a common phrase bandied about among Christians today: "God will never give you more than you can handle." While this pious-sounding statement is generally meant to encourage, it is not an accurate quote from the Bible. Paul writes in 1 Corinthians 10, "God is faithful, and he will not let you be tempted beyond your ability, but with the temptation he will also provide the way of escape, that you may be able to endure it." It isn't even accurate to say that God will never give you more temptation than you can handle, for God does not tempt anyone – James 1:13.

The oft used phrase is meant to suggest that the hardships, pains, discomforts, disappointments, sorrows and concerns of this life will never be more than 'we can handle'. In light of what the Bible really says, we may need to adjust our sense reality a bit.

The fact is that God can, and often does, give us more than we can handle. It is only then, when our hands and hearts cannot carry the load, that the illusion of self-power and self-reliance and self-achievement come crashing down and we see (again) that it is our God who handles our troubles and sorrows. Were we able to handle all that this sinful world, the devil and our own sinful desires are able to throw at us, what need would we have of God? Were we able to cure all ills, what need would we have of our healing Savior? Were we to defeat all evil men and stop all crime, what need would we have to love our enemies?

This sin-filled life is more than we can handle and God wants us to fully rely on Him. He created us to be cared for by Himself, loved by Himself, and in relationship with Himself. Were we self-reliant creatures, we would have no need for God. We do have independence – this lesson is not meant to suggest we do not – but when we assert our independence against God we always fail miserably. Dependency with God is meant to not only provide for our salvation but also to demonstrate just how much God loves us every day and in every way.

When it comes to temptation we have the rich promise of God that he does not allow temptation beyond our ability and that he promises a way out – every single time. Key to grasping this promise of God are three things. 1) Do we recognize something as a temptation? 2) When we recognize something as temptation do we call out to God for the way out? 3) When we know the way out, do we take it – even though it may not seem a desirable way out?

Question

1. What was the way out for these people and did they take it? If not, why not? What can their reasons and reasoning teach us about how we face temptation?

1. Adam and Eve (Genesis 3) _____

2. David (1 Samuel 24) _____

3. David (2 Samuel 11) _____

4. Daniel (Daniel 3) _____

5. Disciples (Matthew 26:36-45) _____

6. Peter (Matthew 26:69-75) _____

7. Ananias and Sapphira (Acts 5) _____

13

2 Kings 6:16 "Fear not, for those who are with us are more than those who are with them."

Read first: 2 Kings 6:8-19

This particular "Fear not!" does not come directly from God, but it does come from someone in very close contact. Elisha, the prophet of God, says "Fear not!" to his servant and then he prays that God would demonstrate why the servant should not be afraid. God opens the eyes of the young man and "he saw, and behold, the mountain was full of horses and chariots of fire all around Elisha."

The text opens up the opportunity to ask several questions. First, did Elisha know that the king of Syria was coming? Elisha knew, or was told by God, the other destinations of the Syrian army. Second, did Elisha see the army of God or did he simply trust in its existence? Third, if Elisha did see the army of God, what does this say about the relationship between God and his prophets? Did God give special sight of the present as well as visions of the future to his called servants? As God pulls back the curtain between this world and the spiritual world, what type of clarity may we expect? Perhaps the question Jesus asked is pertinent here, "If I have told you earthly things and you do not believe, how can you believe if I tell you heavenly things?"

Greater than the answers to these questions is the possibility that we may better understand God saying, "Fear not, I am with you!" God is one, indeed, but his army is a multitude of multitudes. Where God goes, so too go his angels (note how angels were ready at the beck and call of Jesus) and if God is with us, what need we fear?

Importantly, God opens the eyes of the servant – what a measure of grace for him and a lesson for us! God prizes faith – the conviction of things not seen – but he is merciful to our sinfully limited condition and from time to time shares things nearly too wonderful for us to comprehend. In this case with the servant of Elisha, we can "Fear not!" because we too are loved by God and surrounded by his presence, power and protection.

Prayer: Ask your Father in heaven to remind you to have faith when what you see around you is nothing but disaster, or destruction, or danger.

> "But as for the good things of this life, and its ills, God has willed that these should be common to both; that we might not too eagerly covet the things which wicked men are seen equally to enjoy, nor shrink with an unseemly fear from the ills which even good men often suffer."
> – Augustine, City of God, Book 1

Diving In

"God opens the eyes of the young man and 'he saw, and behold, the mountain was full of horses and chariots of fire all around Elisha.'"

For now we see in a mirror dimly, but then face to face. Now I know in part; then I shall know fully, even as I have been fully known. (1 Corinthians 13:12)

Theology

We do not see all there is with our eyes. Some things are too small to see without magnification, some things are too far away to see without a telescope, and some things are beyond our vision and must be revealed. Paul told of this truth thousands of years ago in his letter to the church at Corinth.

We do not know the full reason why God limited our vision the way He did, but perhaps it is because to see-all would be to know-all and we simply cannot handle such knowledge – especially in our sin-sickened condition. Yet God does grant expanded vision from time to time. He does because of His mercy and His love for us – not because we necessarily need to see. God desires to have us believe without seeing (this is faith) because this belief places all our trust in the One true God.

Faith, then, is a difficult thing. We tend to rely upon those things and people which we see often. But God is a spirit and invisible to our earthly eyes. (See 1 Timothy 1:17.) We are commanded to have no other gods – other than the One we cannot see. We can certainly see where he has been, though. We see God in all that has been made. We see God in the majestic working of all things – from the rotation of the galaxies to the development of the unborn child. We saw Jesus – well, those who lived two thousand years ago did – but he has been taken from our sight. We are given the most wonderful gift: a faith which saves us through Jesus, a faith which heals, and a faith which can move mountains.

Question

Many times in the Bible we read that God opened eyes. Fill in the chart below. Not all instances of open eyes will fit well in the chart. Sometimes people prayed for God to open *His* eyes. In these cases, what did the people hope God saw? If God did "open his eyes" what did He see? The last line is for you to fill in for yourself.

	Persons Involved	What they wanted to see	What/Who opened the eyes	Result of opened eyes
Genesis 3:1-7				
Genesis 21:19				
Numbers 22				
1 Kings 8:29, 52				
2 Kings 6:17-20				
Nehemiah 1:6				

	Persons Involved	What they wanted to see	What/Who opened the eyes	Result of opened eyes
Proverbs 20:13				
Jeremiah 32:16-20				
Daniel 9:18				
Matthew 9:30				
Mark 8:22-26				
Luke 24:31				
John 9				
Acts 9:8-18				
– You –				

14

2 Kings 19:6, Isaiah 37:6 "Fear not because of the words that you have heard, with which the servants of the king of Assyria have reviled me."

Read first: 2 Kings 19:1-7

The children's song, "Sticks and stones may break my bones, but words will never hurt me." is only partially correct. Words do hurt; they hurt the spirit and the psyche. Words can make a person ill, or make them tremble; words can also encourage, make a person smile and laugh.

King Hezekiah and the people of Jerusalem are hurt by the words sent to them from the king of Assyria, but God's perspective is most revealing. Literally the text says, "Do not be afraid of the words which you heard which the servants of the king of Assyria blasphemed me." Essentially, God heard the king of Assyria and He really didn't like what was said – about Him!

This entire story is about who is hearing whom. Hezekiah hears Sennacherib. Hezekiah hears God. God has heard Sennacherib. Sennacherib hears Hezekiah. Hezekiah hears back from Sennacherib. Hezekiah talks to God who hears him. God talks to Hezekiah. And strangely enough, neither Hezekiah, Sennacherib, nor God actually are in the same room at the same time – All this talking is going on through messengers! This is a story of how, though God is not 'physically' present, He is nonetheless 'entirely' present and hears all the conversations. Clearly God does not take lightly all that has been said against Him. The story ends with the Assyrian army dead outside of Jerusalem and Sennacherib dead in his 'church' at home.

If we are honest, we see (and hear) plenty of blaspheming going on all around us today but few dead bodies show up unexpectedly (at least ones we can connect with blaspheming God). Perhaps God is more patient now with the coming of His son Jesus, or perhaps all things are being stored up for the final judgement. Either way, the "Fear Not!" in this passage compliments the idea that if God is for us, who can be against us? If we are with God, and God is reviled and blasphemed, He will take care of that, and take care of protecting us as well. Words meant to harm us and tear down our great God should drive us to our knees – in prayer. We should never think that God cannot or will not hear us for if God hears the evil against him, will He not much more turn his ear to his children whom he loves? Yes, and Amen!

Prayer: Praise your heavenly Father with words given to you in the Scriptures. Speak to other believers in psalms and spiritual songs.

Diving In

"Clearly God does not take lightly all that has been said against him."

I tell you, on the day of judgment people will give account for every careless word they speak, for by your words you will be justified, and by your words you will be condemned. (Matthew 12:36)

Theology

God hears all. It is a Biblical truth. Whether it is God's listening to Sennacherib and Hezekiah, or Jesus telling us that accounting will be had for every careless word; whether it is God listening to Pharaoh and to Nebuchadnezzar or Jesus perceiving the thoughts of the Pharisees, the Bible is clear – God hears all.

God hears all. This is a scary truth. Our mouths are a restless evil, happy to spill out venom and vile. James holds no punches when he describes the tongue as a forest on fire, a world of unrighteousness, full of deadly poison; it stains the body, sets life on fire and is itself set on fire by hell. With the mouth we quarrel, we gossip, we curse, and we covet. The thought that we are held accountable for every careless word is as frightening as our words are damning.

Yet God hears more than evil. God hears our prayers! "I love the LORD, because he has heard my voice and my pleas for mercy. Because he inclined his ear to me, therefore I will call on him as long as I live." "Come and hear, all you who fear God, and I will tell what he has done for my soul. I cried to him with my mouth, and high praise was on my tongue. If I had cherished iniquity in my heart, the Lord would not have listened. But truly God has listened; he has attended to the voice of my prayer."

The most wonderful aspect of prayer, beyond the fact that God hears prayer, is that prayer is a conversation between a loving Father and a dear child. The Son of God taught that the proper way to begin prayer is to say, "Our Father in heaven". Moreover we are encouraged and even commanded to converse with our Father in heaven. We speak after we have heard what he has said in his love letters to us (a.k.a. the Bible); we listen to his will written on our hearts as we learn to speak to him with words he has already given us.

Yes, God hears all. All the more reason to make a habit of speaking wisely!

Question

Many times in the Bible we read that God heard or listened. Fill in the chart below with some of the notable times God heard, or promised to hear, something. The last line is for you to fill in for yourself.

	Persons Involved	What God heard	How God felt about what he heard	God's Plans
Genesis 4:10				
Genesis 18:20				
Exodus 2:23				
Deuteronomy 24:14-15				
Judges 3:15				

	Persons Involved	What God heard	How God felt about what he heard	God's Plans
1 Kings 17:20-24				
Psalm 107				
Matthew 15:21-28				
– You –				

15

Psalm 49:16 "Fear not when a man becomes rich, when the glory of his house increases."

Read first: Psalm 49

Most people are probably not very afraid when someone becomes rich. Generally we are happy for them, though our sinful nature wishes we were the ones floating in money. We all have our own life, our own level of riches. Some people use their funds to drive a 'nicer' car than others or to live in a 'larger' home or have more expensive 'toys'. The talents, as Jesus calls them, that have been entrusted to each of us are ours; our neighbor's talents are his. We are called to account for our two talents, not our neighbor's five.

Still, this "Fear Not!" is written for a reason. Looking at Psalm 49 as a whole we see a psalm dedicated to proper perspective on earthly wealth and eternal life. Basically this is a 'you can't take it with you when you die' psalm. True enough. Still, what's to be afraid of? Well, verses 5 and 6 help out a bit.

"Why should I fear in times of trouble, when the iniquity of those who cheat me surrounds me, those who trust in their wealth and boast of the abundance of their riches?"

Interestingly, a historical connection may be made to the the Spanish Inquisition, when the king and queen were plundering and murdering their citizens (in the name of Christ) to become absurdly wealthy. People would try to buy their way out of the torture chambers or would sell their land and possessions in order to escape the country. As a Spaniard in 1492 many people "feared in times of trouble, when the iniquity [of Ferdinand, Isabella and de Torquemada] surrounded" them.

Immoral rich people can be scary but this psalm teaches us to see beyond the wealth, which is temporary, and beyond our poverty, which is temporary, to the eternal destination of each and every person (the wise, the fool and the evil). Fear shortens our vision, trust expands it. The rich man will die but then what of his soul? The poor man will die but then what of his soul? If we are rich or poor, we ask our Father in heaven for the wisdom necessary to live in such a fearless way so that when we die, we may go to the 'generation of my fathers' for whom "the Lord God is their light and they reign forever and ever."

Prayer: Talk with your Father in heaven about how the love of money is the root of all evil and ask Him to renew your love for Him only.

Diving In

"Most people are probably not very afraid when someone becomes rich. Generally we are happy for them, though our sinful nature wishes we were the ones floating in money. We all have our own life, our own level of riches."

Question

1. Who are some of the rich people in the Bible? Did they use their wealth for good or for ill?

Verse	Person	Good or ill?
Genesis 13:2		
Genesis 26:12		
1 Chronicles 29:28		
2 Chronicles 9:22		
2 Chronicles 32:26-28		
Matthew 19:16-22		
Matthew 27:57		
Luke 19:1-9		

Theology

There are a ton of verses in the Bible about money. And not just about money as a thing but verses about spending, lending, interest, debt, responsibility, and giving. Money is a vast topic for study and application in every person's life. Here is one passage which frames a fundamentally correct approach to money. See if your financial life, viewpoint and practice fits inside of it – if it does not, it is certainly time to change.

> God is able to make all grace abound to you, so that having all sufficiency in all things at all times, you may abound in every good work. [TRUST] As it is written, "He has distributed freely, he has given to the poor; his righteousness endures forever." He who supplies seed to the sower and bread for food will supply and multiply your seed for sowing and increase the harvest of your righteousness. [FREEDOM] You will be enriched in every way to be generous in every way, which through us will produce thanksgiving to God. [GENEROSITY] For the ministry of this service is not only supplying the needs of the saints but is also overflowing in many thanksgivings to God. [TITHE] (2 Corinthians 9:8–12)

TRUST is a cornerstone of money because all money and all material goods come from God. As the Good-Giver God entrusts his children with material things; not always as they want, but always as they need. We trust that God is able and willing to provide, either in advance or right on time, for all of our needs and in such a way that His Name is glorified.

FREEDOM is a cornerstone because we see that wealth comes from God's abundance, not our own attempts to gain possessions through indebtedness to people or institutions. Debt is unhealthy and unwise. Debt shows irresponsibility, lack of foresight and leads to poverty and ruin. Debt says, "I will make my own supply and multiply my own goods under the illusion of increase."

GENEROSITY is a cornerstone because it reflects the nature of the Giver of all good things. As God is, he desires that we be also – he forgives abundantly and so should we; he loves passionately and so should we; he is enriches us and we should enrich others.

TITHE is a cornerstone because it demonstrates the priority of the Gospel of Jesus Christ. In the New Testament age tithe does not have a numerical value. Rather, tithing today means supporting God's church and mission here on earth to save lost souls, bring comfort to the needy and justice to the oppressed.

16

Psalm 55:19 "God will give ear and humble them, he who is enthroned from of old, because they do not change and they fear not God."

Read first: Psalm 55:16-19

This "Fear not!" is a bit different from the rest, although it is identical in the Hebrew text to the others in this devotional. In English we lose a bit of the impact simply through our grammatical construction. In the original this verse reads more like: "God hears and humbles them, He the Ever-Residing/Present-One, because they change not, they fear not God."

The idea to fear God presents an interesting counterpoint. So far, we have heard that we are to not fear evil, the future, enemies, God's holiness, or rich people. Now we read, by extension, that we should fear God. It is kind of confusing, how fear on the one hand is unhealthy and rebuked by God, but how on the other hand it seems to be a necessary attitude when facing God. In fact, in the case of Gideon and God's holiness, where

Gideon felt that he would die because he saw God, God did not tell him to not be afraid of God, simply that he did not need to fear dying because God had decided to be merciful. Gideon's natural reaction and attitude toward God were good and proper.

Often children are taught that when the Bible says 'Fear God' it means 'have a healthy respect for God'. This definition is not the fullest we can provide, however. The Bible teaches us to be afraid of God's wrath and anger, to be scared of the just punishment for our sins, to tremble before God. Psalm 2:11 "Serve the Lord with fear, and rejoice with trembling." Philippians 2:12 "Work out your own salvation with fear and trembling, for it is God who works in you." Sometimes this offends the sensibilities of New Testament Christians who see God in Jesus as only the Friend, the Lamb, the Lover of Souls. We forget that the "Son of Man" will send souls to "eternal punishment" (Matthew 25); that "The Son of Man will send his angels, and they will . . . throw them into the fiery furnace. In that place there will be weeping and gnashing of teeth." (Matthew 13:41) We forget that the Lamb was slaughtered by God for our sins and iniquities.

A very healthy fear of eternal punishment – a fear which drives the soul to the comfort of the forgiveness and grace found in Jesus – is a good thing. Those who do not fear God will be humbled by God, they "will be cast down into the pit of destruction." We should fear hell and eternal damnation; not because we believe we will end up there but because of the fact that these exist for those who deny God. God's justice is frightening. God's solution – the death and resurrection of his son Jesus – is nothing to fear at all.

Prayer: Talk with your Father in heaven about a proper fear of Him.

Diving In

"A very healthy fear of eternal punishment – which drives a soul to the comfort of the forgiveness and grace found in Jesus – is a good thing. Those who do not fear God will be humbled by God, they 'will be cast down into the pit of destruction.' We should fear hell and eternal damnation; not because we believe we will end up there but because of the fact that these exist for those who deny God."

Theology

The Scriptures tell us that God wants all to be saved. In fact, God continually repeats his call to repentance and salvation.

- Have I any pleasure in the death of the wicked, declares the Lord GOD, and not rather that he should turn from his way and live? (Ezekiel 18:23, see also verses 30-32)
- God our Savior desires all people to be saved and to come to the knowledge of the truth. (1 Timothy 2:3–4)
- Jesus came into Galilee, proclaiming the gospel of God, and saying, "The time is fulfilled, and the kingdom of God is at hand; repent and believe in the gospel." (Mark 1:14–15)
- Turn to me and be saved, all the ends of the earth! For I am God, and there is no other. (Isaiah 45:22)
- Therefore say to them, Thus declares the LORD of hosts: Return to me, says the LORD of hosts, and I will return to you, says the LORD of hosts. (Zechariah 1:3)
- Repent and be baptized every one of you in the name of Jesus Christ for the forgiveness of your sins, and you will receive the gift of the Holy Spirit. (Acts 2:38)
- And the Lord said, "I am Jesus . . . open their eyes, so that they may turn from darkness to light and from the power

of Satan to God, that they may receive forgiveness of sins and a place among those who are sanctified by faith in me." (Acts 26:15–18)

The correct teaching about hell, damnation, condemnation, sin, and rebellion against God is that if a person is happy in their sins, pleased to do evil, and unrepentant, it is then that the unrelenting demands of God's Law and his just sentence of punishment and banishment from His presence must be spoken. When a person is convicted of their sin in their heart, they must immediately be assured of the grace and forgiveness of God. They must be shown the love of God in Jesus, forgiven of their sin, and instructed in the life of a child of God.

Question

Is hell a real, scary place? Should we be afraid of it? Examine these passages about that place and about the Judgment of God.

1. Matthew 11:20-24 _____

2. Mark 9:47-48 _____

3. 2 Thessalonians 1:5-10 _____

4. Isaiah 66:15-16 _____

5. Revelation 14:9-11 _____

Theology

The Bible uses a variety of words for what we today call hell. Sheol, Gehenna, and Hades are the most common. Jeremiah uses a physical/temporal place of fire called Topheth/Tophet to illustrate a horrible place of slaughter and death.

In general, Sheol (the Hebrew word) is the place of the dead. Arrival in Sheol was not dependant upon how one lived life – it simply was a word which meant something similar (but not exactly) to 'the grave' as we use that term in English today. There are a couple of instances where Sheol does have the emphasis of a place of exile for those who continue in sin. Hades, the Greek word used to translate the Hebrew Sheol, often carried the same general meaning as Sheol – a place of the dead. It is a place of darkness, desolation and debasement.

There is a terrible place, and some dispute whether it is Sheol/Ghenna or not, which was prepared for the devil and his angels: "Then he will say to those on his left, 'Depart from me, you cursed, into the eternal fire prepared for the devil and his angels.'" Into this place it is promised that sinful people will go: "But as for the cowardly, the faithless, the detestable, as for murderers, the sexually immoral, sorcerers, idolaters, and all liars, their portion will be in the lake that burns with fire and sulfur, which is the second death."

Regardless of the specific nuances of interpretation, the Bible clearly states, and repeatedly states, that there is a terrible and horrible place of punishment and torment for those who have continually rejected the grace and love of God and chosen to live in sinful and despicable ways here on earth. This is the place of God's judgment.

The place of God's mercy, forgiveness and love is heaven, Paradise, and everlasting life. Let us pray that many would know the Lord and join us there!

17

Psalm 91:5 "You will fear not the terror of the night."

Read first: Psalm 91:1-6

This psalm is familiar to many because of the devotional song composed by Michael Joncas, "On Eagles' Wings." And this psalm contains a great many comforting verses. Yet, what is the 'terror of the night' which we are to "Fear not!"?

Two possibilities loom large. First is the destroying angel from 2 Samuel 24:10-17. David had ordered a census and the Lord was angered. A prophet named Gad was sent to give David a choice of three punishments. David chose one and 70,000 Israelites died in three days at the hand of the "angel who was working destruction". The thought of that many people dying in that short amount of time is frightening indeed! The second possibility is the 'destroyer' of the Passover event, which in the Exodus 12 text is synonymous (in all but verse 23) with the Lord. It isn't until Psalm 78 that we have the phrase "destroying angels" to give us a more descriptive picture of who did what on the night the firstborn were slain.

Honestly, both possibilities are scary! Both point to a spiritual being, governed by God, who has the power and authority to instantly end any life, and any number of lives, on this earth. Now, while this death-bringing being is scary, it isn't actually evil because this being is sent from God.

Yet into this reality burns the Word of God: "Fear Not!" My Lord, my Refuge, My Fortress, My God in whom I trust will deliver and protect me from His destroyer. In a way God is protecting us from Himself, much as his forgiveness protects us from the righteous punishment we deserve. God's destroyer-angel is real, his power is real, yet we fear not because we have made the Lord our dwelling place. Those who live with the Lord do not fear – who would want to live anywhere else? A fearless life is located in the presence of the Lord God.

Prayer: Talk with your Father in heaven about making Him your dwelling place.

> "Serve the Lord with gladness. All servitude is full of bitterness: all who are bound to a lot of servitude both are slaves, and discontented. Fear not the servitude of that Lord: there will be no groaning there, no discontent, no indignation; no one seeketh to be sold to another master, since it is a sweet service, because we are all redeemed. Great happiness, brethren, it is, to be a slave in that great house, although in bonds."
> – Augustine, Expositions on the Psalms, Psalm 100

<u>Diving In</u>

"We fear not because we have made the Lord our dwelling place. Those who live with the Lord do not fear – who would want to live anywhere else? A fearless life is located in the presence of the Lord God."

Theology

Meditation is a Bible-prescribed method of hearing, learning and living God's word. Rather than detail some of the theology behind the house of the Lord, let's use this Bible study page to meditate on just five of some of the most beautiful and encouraging passages in the Bible.

If you are unfamiliar with meditating on Scripture, it means to contemplate and reflect on the words and sentences and passages which God preserved for you in the Bible. After spending lengthy time in contemplation, memorize the words. Say the words to yourself many times a day. After you have memorized the words, pray the words to your Father in heaven. Remember, prayer is a conversation so you will want to discuss the words with your Father; tell Him what you feel, ask your questions, seek His wisdom and application in your life.

- Surely goodness and mercy shall follow me all the days of my life, and I shall dwell in the house of the LORD forever.
- One thing have I asked of the LORD, that will I seek after: that I may dwell in the house of the LORD all the days of my life, to gaze upon the beauty of the LORD and to inquire in his temple.

- Blessed is the one O God whom you choose and bring near to dwell in your courts! We shall be satisfied with the goodness of your house, the holiness of your temple!
- Let not your hearts be troubled. Believe in God; believe also in me. In my Father's house are many rooms. If it were not so, would I have told you that I go to prepare a place for you? And if I go and prepare a place for you, I will come again and will take you to myself, that where I am you may be also. And you know the way to where I am going."
- Jesus answered him, "If anyone loves me, he will keep my word, and my Father will love him, and we will come to him and make our home with him."

18

Isaiah 7:4 "Say to him, 'Be careful, be quiet, fear not, and do not let your heart be faint.'"

Read first: Isaiah 7:1-9

This command from God to evil King Ahaz has in the Hebrew the sense of, "Sit down, shut up, and stop being a 'fraidy cat.'" The words are short and consonant heavy; they carry a tone of sharp rebuke. And given who the audience is, this is understandable. A real loser on the list of horrible kings, Ahaz sacrificed his son to other gods, remodeled the temple according to a pagan design, and gave away the riches of Judah to the king of Assyria. It is amazing that God would even bother to speak to him let alone give him words of comfort or encouragement.

However, God isn't acting in kindness toward Ahaz as much as he is honoring the memory of David and to lesser extent Uzziah and Jotham. God is moving to protect the city of Jerusalem and the temple which bears His name. God also uses the event to deliver prophetic words about Syria, Israel, Judah, and most importantly about the coming Savior. So God has more in mind than just a simple word to Ahaz and we should know that God speaks in this way many times in Scripture.

This event is a really good example of God working despite – and in the midst of – evil people. Both kings of the divided people of Israel do not walk with God, the kings and nations of Assyria and Syria certainly do not, and never has Egypt. But God dives in there, protects his chosen people, delivers words of hope mingled with the reality of coming punishment, and sets up signposts that effectively say, "God – This Direction."

The fact that God would speak with evil men – and speak words of hope, peace, or comfort to them – may feel uncomfortable to us. It doesn't bother God, however. Perhaps we see here how God holds out hope, even for the worst of us, that we all might be saved. Perhaps one of the best places for the Light to shine is in the middle of darkness.

Prayer: Ask your heavenly Father to open your eyes to the signposts which say, "God – This Direction."

> "But sometimes even when faith is to be relied upon, youth is not trusted. Use wine, therefore, sparingly, in order that the weakness of the body may not increase, not for pleasurable excitement, for each alike kindles a flame, both wine and youth. Let fasts also put a bridle on tender age, and spare diet restrain the unsubdued appetites with a kind of rein. Let reason check, hope subdue, and fear curb them. For he who knows not how to govern his desires, like a man run away with by wild horses, is overthrown, bruised, torn, and injured."
> – Ambrose, Concerning Virgins, Book III

Diving In

"The fact that God would speak with evil men – and speak words of hope, peace, or comfort to them – may feel uncomfortable to us. It doesn't bother God, however. Perhaps we see here how God holds out hope, even for the worst of us, that we all might be saved. Perhaps one of the best places for the Light to shine is in the middle of darkness."

Question

God does speak to many evil and/or non-believing people in the Bible. To whom did He speak in these passages?

1. Genesis 20 _____

2. Genesis 41:25 _____

3. Numbers 22 _____

4. Daniel 2 _____

5. Daniel 4 _____

6. Jonah 3 _____

7. Isaiah 45 _____

8. Matthew 27:19 _____

Theology

Long ago, at many times and in many ways, God spoke to our fathers by the prophets, but in these last days he has spoken to us by his Son, whom he appointed the heir of all things, through whom also he created the world.

This sentence is from the book of Hebrews, the first verse. It is the 'topic sentence' of the whole book, setting the stage for the reader who may now expect to hear about the words spoken in 'these last days' by Jesus the son of God. Jesus is the last and the greatest prophet, the culmination and the 'Yes' of all God's promises and prophesies. Even though God spoke to non-believers in the past, nothing said to them comes close to what was said by Jesus. This Jesus, the Word of God, is the light and the life of men, and he is full of grace and truth. Our ears do well to listen to Him!

19

Isaiah 8:12 "Fear not what they fear."

Read first: Isaiah 8:11-22

People who are not afraid inspire greater respect than those who are. I recall a passage in the book "Flags of our Fathers" where a company of soldiers landed on an island under a rainstorm of bullets and bombs. Everyone was terrified but one man. This man, the company leader, sat calmly behind a rock, and while bullets and bombs flew all around them, took off his boots and shook the sand out. His companions were astonished at his demeanor and poise; it inspired them and motivated them.

The word of God to Isaiah to, "Fear not what they fear." must have set Isaiah as an oddity in the community, if not the nation. Himself prophesying the frightening destruction of Israel and Judah, and living through attacks and sieges, Isaiah's fearless character would have probably bewildered any of us if we had been living then. How can a man not be afraid when everyone else is? Is he crazy, clueless, or conscious of a reality the rest of us cannot perceive?

A popular television show of the late 20th century portrayed a certain captain of a ship as a man who took risks with near abandon when his friends were around. One day, dismayed at his behavior, one of his friends questioned his predilection for death-defying gambles. "My friend," the captain said in a quiet voice, "I've always known I'll die alone." The captain was making the point that he was conscious of a reality his friends did not comprehend. Isaiah was conscious of a reality, that while proclaimed in the streets and in print, the people of Israel and Judah refused to comprehend. The reality was that God's justice and punishment were swiftly coming. Instead of fearing God, however, the people found other matters to fear, other people to be afraid of, and other potential futures to horrify them.

God's word to Isaiah provided him a powerful adjustment of perception. What others called fearful was not. What God called fearful was fearful. And God called himself, the Lord of hosts, the Fearful One, the Dreadful One. Jesus said the same thing in a different way: "Do not fear those who kill the body but cannot kill the soul. Rather fear him who can destroy both soul and body in hell." What do we fear? Poverty, unemployment, sickness, war, hunger, embarrassment? Do we fear and love God the most?

Prayer: Ask your heavenly Father to teach you to fear and love Him the most.

> "Let us, therefore, fear the judgment which awaits teachers. For a severe judgment will those teachers receive 'who teach, but do not,' and those who take upon them the name of Christ falsely, and say: 'We teach the truth,' and yet go wandering about idly, and exalt themselves, and make their boast in the mind of the flesh."
> – Clement, The First Epistle of the Blessed Clement

Diving In

"God's word to Isaiah provided him a powerful adjustment of perception. What others called fearful was not. What God called fearful was fearful. And God called himself, the Lord of hosts, the Fearful One, the Dreadful One. Jesus said the same thing in a different way: 'Do not fear those who kill the body but cannot kill the soul. Rather fear him who can destroy both soul and body in hell.' What do we fear?"

Question

What do we fear? Here are some things God does not want us to fear or be anxious about:

1. Proverbs 12:25 _____

2. Matthew 6:31

    a. _____

    b. _____

    c. _____

3. Matthew 6:34 _____

4. Matthew 10:19 _____

5. Luke 10:41 _____

6. Philippians 4:6 _____

7. 2 Corinthians 11:23-12:10 _____

8. Hebrews 13:6 _____

20

Isaiah 10:24 "Thus says the Lord GOD of hosts: 'O my people, who dwell in Zion, fear not the Assyrians when they strike.'"

Read first: Isaiah 10:20-27

Have you ever had the experience where your doctor/nurse says, "Don't worry, this will only hurt a little bit." before the needle plunges painfully into your body and injects a seemingly endless amount of medicine? God tells his people to "Fear not!" even though a whole bunch of them will be presently wiped out by the Assyrians. Of course, God has the bigger picture in mind here and so too the doctor with the needle. The doctor sees how the needle prick is a small event as compared to the great illness the medicine prevents. God sees how this Assyrian strike is but a small event in the history of his people. God says as much in these words, "In a very little while my fury will come to an end."

God also knows that he will not only wipe the Assyrians out later but he will also preserve a remnant of Israel, bring the remnant back and prosper it in due time. Does this revelation help ease the apprehension of the coming invasion? Do the doctor's words help ease the pain caused by the needle? What is the real fear of the needle? Is it the prick or the fear that the pain will not end? What is the real fear of the Assyrian attack? Is it the soldiers who will be lost or the thought that the Assyrians will completely destroy every man, woman and child? (Perhaps there is the greater fear that God in his great anger will wipe every one of his children off the face of the earth.)

God points to the correct thing to fear when he says, "My fury will come to an end, and my anger will be directed to their destruction." The Assyrians, though wicked and powerful, though allowed and directed by God to punish Israel for idolatry and covenant-breaking, do not and will not have the last laugh, so to speak. The Assyrians are not all powerful, God the Lord of Hosts is all powerful. And God's fury is not everlasting, it will come to an end.

Fear not the armies of men, is what God is saying, for though they be present and powerful, they are never beyond the immediate control of the All Mighty God of heaven and earth. Neither is the wrath of God an endless source of destruction. The grace, mercy, love and forgiveness of God will rise up and quiet the righteous anger of God.

Prayer: Talk with your Father in heaven and ask Him for a proper perspective on the events of this day.

Diving In

"The Assyrians, though wicked and powerful, though allowed and directed by God to punish Israel for idolatry and covenant-breaking, do not and will not have the last laugh, so to speak. The Assyrians are not all powerful, God the Lord of Hosts is all powerful."

Theology

Who were the Assyrians? The Assyrians were a major player in Biblical history. They are mentioned in over 100 Bible verses, from the first book of the Bible to the second to last book in the Old Testament! Most references are in 2 Kings, 2 Chronicles and Isaiah; the time when Assyria had the most dominance in the Middle East. Although their empire waxed and waned, the modern-day location of Iraq is where Assyria was centralized most of the time.

Question

1. Who were some of the most famous kings of Assyria?
    a. 2 Kings 15:19:29 / 1 Chronicles 5:6

    _____

    b. 2 Kings 17 _____

    c. 2 Kings 18 - 19 _____

2. How did God first feel about the people in the capital of Assyria?
    a. Jonah _____

3. How did God feel about Nineveh 100 years later?
    a. Nahum _____

4. What were God's plans for the nations he used to punish Israel for their idolatry?

    a. Isaiah 14:24-27

    b. Jeremiah 50:17-20

5. Consider the close literary connection between the prophesy about the coming Messiah and the dominance of the nation of Israel – illustrated through the nation of Assyria. Is it any wonder that the disciples of Jesus thought he would reign in Jerusalem?

    a. Micah 5

21

Isaiah 35:4 "Fear not! Behold your God will come."

Read first: Isaiah 35:1-7

We must read this chapter in Isaiah with the presupposition that it has been, at least partially, fulfilled in Jesus the Christ. This interpretation is not something man made up. Rather, Jesus declared to John the Baptist in Luke 7 that these words had been fulfilled. In light of this truth, we hear this "Fear not!" as a call to courage because the victory is assured and the salvation of God is at hand.

God has come in Jesus Christ and the Father has with a vengeance placed upon his son the sins of the world. We need not fear for our sins have been carried by Another. This one and only son has suffered for these sins and died to vanquish them. We need not fear for our sins have been paid for by Another. This incarnate son of God rose from the dead after three days declaring defeat for the devil and death. We need not fear for our salvation is accomplished by Another.

We fear not the world, nor the devil, nor sinful things because our God has come and is coming again. Many things will attempt to cause anxiousness in our heart: wars, threats of war, sickness and disease, injustice and persecution, natural disasters and shortages of resources. Yet we must live with this on our lips: "I fear not! My God will come and save me!" Any other approach to life would accuse our Lord God of lying or of exaggerating – for it is he who has said, "Fear not!" and "I am coming soon!"

Prayer: Talk with your Father in heaven about His salvation through His son Jesus.

> "Beloved, I must explain to you what it is to be 'simple as doves, and wise as serpents.' Now if the simplicity of doves be commendable, what does the wisdom of the serpent have to do with the simplicity of the dove? I love this about the dove: she has no gall; this I fear in the serpent, that he has poison. But now do not fear the serpent altogether; he has something for thee to hate, and something for thee to imitate. For when the serpent is weighed down with age, and he feels the burden of his many years, he contracts and forces himself into a hole, and lays aside his old coat of skin, that he may spring forth into new life. Imitate him in this, thou Christian, who dost hear the Apostle Paul saying to thee, 'Put ye off the old man with his deeds, and put ye on the new man.'"
> – Augustine: Sermons on Selected Lessons, Sermon XIV

Diving In

"Yet we must live with this on our lips: 'I fear not! My God will come and save me!' Any other approach to life would accuse our Lord God of lying or of exaggerating – for it is he who has said, 'Fear not!' and 'I am coming soon!'"

Theology

The coming of God and His Messiah is a constant theme in the Bible. Throughout the entire Old Testament the promises and prophesies about the Coming One are repeated. Then, in the first four books of the New Testament, we meet Him Who Has Come . . . then he leaves again. But, he promises to return! Evidently, the history of the world is not yet complete and so we must wait for the Messiah to return.

Interestingly, Jesus the Messiah did, on the one hand, leave. On the other hand, he is still here! This 'both here and gone', or as it is also described: 'the now and the not yet', can be one of the most puzzling aspects to the Christian faith. It can also be one of the most comforting. Theologians have debated over the previous centuries whether Jesus is present here and in heaven in spiritual form, physical form, or both. The weight of Biblical evidence lies with the answer 'both'; that is, Christ Jesus is present with us in Word and by the power of the Holy Spirit and he is present in heaven at the right hand of God. Christ Jesus is also present with us in his Supper and in our bodies as we have died to sin and Christ lives in us, yet Christ Jesus is also physically ascended and present at the right hand of God the Father.

The point is that wherever we are, here or in heaven, Jesus is with us, really with us, really in us, because he really died and rose for us!

Question

1. How does Jesus promise he will return?
    a. Matthew 16:17
    b. Matthew 24:30
    c. Mark 13:24-27
    d. John 14:3
2. How does Jesus promise he will never leave?
    a. Matthew 18:20
    b. Matthew 28:20
3. How do we know Jesus has physically left?
    a. Mark 16:19
    b. Luke 24:51
    c. Acts 1:9-11
4. How do we know Jesus is physically here?
    a. Galatians 2:19 (If we have died and Christ lives in us, is he not physically present as we are physically present?)
    b. 1 Corinthians 11:23-27 (If the body and blood were only symbolic or only present at the Last Supper, why/how would someone be guilty of sinning against them?)

22

Isaiah 41:10 "Fear not, for I am with you; I am your God."

Isaiah 41:13 "I, the LORD your God, say to you, 'Fear not, I am the one who helps you.'"

Isaiah 41:14 "Fear not, you worm Jacob."

Read first: Isaiah 41:8-16

The call to "Fear Not!" in Isaiah 41 is based on God's eternal status and all powerful nature. Because He was first before all, because he currently is over all and because he will be the last, God's people are to not fear.

To comprehend God's argument here (and it is posed as a type of legal argument) is quite difficult. We don't understand eternal existence. We don't know what it means to control people and nations without misstep. We cannot help in any and every circumstance, cannot be present at all times and in all places, cannot place ourselves above other persons or other peoples claiming the title 'Creator'. The foundation of God's argument is beyond our ability to fathom, and in many ways this is precisely why we may have confidence in our God and draw comfort from his command to "Fear not!"

This is a true statement: Nothing can separate us from the love of God in Christ Jesus, nothing! The past cannot separate us from God for God has always been present. Therefore we may look at history and know that we will find God there. There is no place on earth we can go to escape God. Therefore we may know that location does not separate us from God. And since God is eternal, when nations rise and fall, when nature turns on its head, we may rest in the peace which teaches God began to help us long before we got to this point in time and God will continue to be with us forever.

Three times in this passage from Isaiah God tell us to "Fear Not!" This emphasis teaches us that God feels that this state of being – living in fearlessness – is extremely important for us to grasp. Fear turns our eyes and heart from God. Fear pushes God away when he comes to help. Let's instead live the life God calls us to – fearing the Lord and fearless of all other things.

Prayer: Meditate with your Father in heaven on your mortality and
His eternal nature.

Diving In

"Because He was first before all, because he currently is over all and because he will be the last, God's people are to not fear."

Theology

When it comes to the teaching about God, we can divide what God reveals about Himself in the Bible into three large categories: Knowledge of God (how we know Him); Nature of God (what constitutes God and what qualities does God have); Trinity of God (when God is both one and three).

The qualities of God are known as his attributes. God's attributes are those things which identify him, describe him and speak to his character. Some of God's most well know attributes are: eternal, omniscient, living, holy, righteous, truth, love, and all-powerful (omnipotent).

God describes and details his eternal character in a variety of ways. Eternal means to not be limited by time. When applied to God, eternal carries the idea that God had no beginning and no end; He is eternal because he was always outside of time. When applied to creatures, like humanity and angels, it means that while we had a beginning, we will have no end because God will remove the limitation of time from us. Thus we will have eternal life – and in a very real sense, God is the eternal life which we will have.

Question

    How does God describe and detail his eternal attribute in these Scripture passages?

1. Job 38:4-7 _____

2. Exodus 3:14 _____

3. Isaiah 41:4, 48:12 _____

4. Isaiah 43:10 _____

5. John 8:58 _____

6. Revelation 1:8 _____

7. Psalm 90:1-4 _____

8. 1 Timothy 6:17 _____

23

Isaiah 43:1 "Fear not, for I have redeemed you."

Isaiah 43:5 "Fear not, for I am with you."

Read first: Isaiah 43:1-7

Isaiah 43 is a love letter from God to his chosen people. Or at least it seems so at first. In the beginning He is gracious, passionate, demonstrative. But then God extols his eternal and benevolent character and contrasts it with Israel/Jacob's relentless pursuit of sinful living. He promises forgiveness yet at the same time destruction. He promises salvation yet at the same time suffering. It is like God is wrestling with his love and his disdain for his people. Which will win out?

The two "Fear not!" phrases come in the beginning, when everything seems gentle and peaceful. Or at least that is the sense one gets with a superficial reading. Digging deeper, the picture is not so nice. Sure, God promises his presence in verse 2 and 5, and sure, God claims his people in verse 1 and 4 and 7. However, God also promises that his people will be ransomed, released and returned. But a person cannot be ransomed if they are not first captured, cannot be released unless they are first imprisoned; cannot be returned if they are not first taken. God is with you when, not if, you pass through the waters and the fire. God ransoms you when you are found to be captive. God brings his people home only after they have been spread across the face of the earth in exile.

This is not a cheery walk down the garden lane with breezes blowing and flower petals fluttering. This is a tortured hike to exile; it is banishment and punishment. And along this very long road, remember: "Fear Not!" God is with you, God has redeemed you.

But surely there must be an easier way, a better way, to deal with sin . . . right? Must fear-inducing calamity come? Must God reassure us before the disaster that He will be there in the disaster and we should "Fear not!" – can't he just make it all not happen? Ten more chapters along, Isaiah will foretell the easier, better way. One will come and bear the sin of many, be oppressed and afflicted, carry our sorrows and be despised by us. In truth, however, this other way wasn't really easier, but it was better.

Prayer: Talk with your Father in heaven about how trials may seem to make your life harder but how they actually make your relationship with Him better.

Diving In

"Isaiah 43 is a love letter from God to his chosen people."

Theology

God is love. God loves. And love is a verb! God is passionate about his love and not embarrassed to tell of his love. (God is also a jealous lover, not wanting those he loves to love any one or any thing else.) When taken together, the passages of God's expression of love tell a passionate tale of devotion, desire, joy and tenderness. Take the time to enjoy the love God has for you by meditating (we discussed how to meditate before) on these passages.

1. Isaiah 43:4
2. Isaiah 66:12-14
3. Hosea 2:19-20
4. Hosea 11:1-4
5. Jeremiah 31:3-4
6. Deuteronomy 7:6-9
7. Deuteronomy 32:10-13
8. Matthew 23:37

24

Isaiah 44:2 "Fear not!"

Read first: Isaiah 44:1-5

This "Fear Not!" comes with a unique reference to God's Spirit. The hearers of Isaiah's proclamation were to not fear in their time because of the promise of future blessings and prosperity. Of all the "Fear Not!" statements in the Old Testament, this is one where we see a direct fulfillment by Jesus as the Gospel writer John writes in the 14th chapter of his book.

Does it (or would it) help to know that your present suffering will not be endured by your descendants? Does it make it more bearable to know that a great grandchild (or greater) will have a special blessing given to them by God? For most parents and grandparents, this is the case. We, as good and loving parents, would rather suffer ourselves than have our children suffer. This is not a self-righteous attitude, but one of love for our offspring. The knowledge of a blessing to be given to our descendants is rewarding and inspiring; it helps us see beyond the ills of today to a brighter future.

Today we have the Spirit of God who "helps us in our weakness" and "intercedes for us" and "pours God's love into our hearts" and "searches everything" and "leads us" and "is our guarantee". God's Spirit is the antithesis of fear. This is a really good gift from God because in the New Testament age we are promised future tribulation, such great tribulation as to warrant the words, "And if those days had not been cut short, no human being would be saved." (Matthew 24:22) In light of this prophesy, having the assurance of God's all powerful and all present and ever-working Spirit gives great comfort.

This "Fear not!" is ironic, then, because Isaiah's listeners were not to fear their present troubles because God would pour out his Spirit on a future people who needed this Spirit to endure their present (and future) troubles. So, we may conclude that trouble may always abound on this earth, but God is with his servants, start to finish.

Prayer: Talk with your Father in heaven about your family and how faith is a heritage you can work to pass on.

> "Again, by Moses, He commands 'two young pigeons or a pair of turtle-doves to be offered for sin;' thus saying, that the harmlessness and innocence and placable nature of these tender young birds are acceptable to God, and explaining that like is an expiation for like. Further, the timorousness of the turtle-doves typifies fear in reference to sin."
> – Clement of Alexandria, The Instructor, Book 1

Diving In

"Today we have the Spirit of God who 'helps us in our weakness' and 'intercedes for us' and 'pours God's love into our hearts' and 'searches everything' and 'leads us' and 'is our guarantee'."

Theology

The teaching of the Holy Spirit, who is the third person of the Trinity, fills volumes of study. Ever since the days of the early church, the Holy Spirit has been enjoyed because of His presence, and examined in the light of the Scriptures. A testimony of faith from the early church, now called the Nicene Creed, had in its first version (325 A.D.) this to say about the Holy Spirit:

"We believe in the Holy Ghost."

Obviously not the longest statement on the person and the work of the Holy Spirit! But in 325 A.D. the church was battling false teaching about Jesus, not the Holy Spirit. It was 56 years later when the church met in the city of Constantinople that a fuller statement about the Holy Spirit had to be made in order to refute other false teachings. This is what they had to say in the second version of the Nicene Creed:

"We believe in the Holy Ghost, the Lord and Giver of life, who proceeds from the Father, who with the Father and the Son together is worshiped and glorified, who spake by the prophets. In one holy catholic and apostolic Church; we acknowledge one baptism for the remission of sins; we look for the resurrection of the dead, and the life of the world to come. Amen."

This statement of faith has since, in almost unaltered form, been learned and spoken by the Christian church the world over. If you think about it, that is a stunning accomplishment – to draft a statement which would stand the test of time and examination for nearly 2,000 years around the globe! Of course, since this statement is but a restatement of the Scriptures, it is no wonder it remains to this day.

Question

Where did the authors of the Nicene Creed get their understandings of the Holy Spirit?

1. Is this Spirit holy?

    a. Acts 5:3-4 _____

    b. 1 Corinthians 3:16 _____

2. Is this Spirit a part of baptism?

    a. 1 Corinthians 6:11 _____

    b. Titus 3:5 _____

3. Is this Spirit and the church connected?

    a. Ephesians 2:19-22 _____

    b. Ephesians 4:3-6 _____

4. Is this Spirit connected with the resurrection?

     a. Revelation 14:13 _____

     b. Romans 8:11 _____

5. Is this Spirit from the Father and Son?

     a. John 15:26 _____

     b. John 14:26 _____

6. Did this Spirit speak through the prophets?

     a. Acts 1:16 _____

     b. Isaiah 61:1 _____

25

Isaiah 51:7 "Fear not the reproach of men."

Read first: Isaiah 51:7-8

Righteousness, comfort and the necessity to live with fearless attitudes; these are the themes of Isaiah 51. The heart of the chapter, indeed the middle of it, says, "I, I am he who comforts you; who are you that you are afraid of man who dies, of the son of man who is made like grass, and have forgotten the LORD, your Maker, who stretched out the heavens and laid the foundations of the earth, and you fear continually all the day because of the wrath of the oppressor, when he sets himself to destroy?"

God's point of view is so unique, so refreshing. "I comfort you, I made everything – why are you afraid and why do you fear so ridiculously?" Why are we afraid so often? Perhaps it is because we have become accustomed to a way of looking at life – shortsightedly – and we haven't become acquainted with the alternative, and better, way of perception. Consider when we come under disaster, or drought, or disease, or dictatorship. When these happen we despair and wonder when they will end. Our eyes are on the hardship and not the One who delivers from hardship. We are seeing with our human eyes and not with our God given faith, wisdom and understanding. We see the now, not the not-yet. We think that this present darkness is never ending because we can do nothing to change it. We fail to expect God to change things in the right time. We even, perhaps, fail to take advantage of the comfort God offers in the midst of the 'wrath of the oppressor'.

Honestly, we are so precious to God and so protected by Him. Our hearts are small but they are loved more than all of creation – for creation will pass away but everlasting joy will be upon our heads. Our fears are small and silly yet the Lord of all recognizes our misperception and frailty and calls out to us to "Fear not!"

What is eternity to a mortal? What is light to the unborn? What is the absence of evil? What is the joy of the Lord? In a word, it is trust. Those who trust in the Lord are those who fear not.

Prayer: Talk with your Father in heaven about seeing the world and events with His eyes, from His perspective.

Diving In

"The heart of the chapter, indeed the middle of it, says, 'I, I am he who comforts you; who are you that you are afraid of man who dies, of the son of man who is made like grass, and have forgotten the LORD, your Maker, who stretched out the heavens and laid the foundations of the earth.'"

Question

What is a human? What is mankind? Are we the result of molecules accidentally joining together to make interdependent working systems over eons of time? God tells us who we are, over and over again, so it is very easy to answer these questions and to refute the lies. However, one cannot have knowledge or refute foolishness unless that person has a solid hold on the truth. Use these passages to get a firm foundation.

Humanity is:

1. Designed and made: Genesis 2:7, Psalm 139:13-15
2. Product of the environment: Genesis 3:19
3. More than chemicals and compounds: Ecclesiastes 12:7, Isaiah 42:5, Zechariah 12:1
4. Fragile and short lived: Isaiah 40:6-8, Psalm 102:11, Psalm 144:4
5. Mortal: Genesis 2:17, Genesis 5:5, Matthew 10:28
6. In need of constant strengthening: Psalm 109:24, Isaiah 35:1, Luke 4:2, John 4:6
7. Constrained to only decades of life: Psalm 90:10, Genesis 6:3
8. Destined to be bodily resurrected: Romans 6:5, 1 Corinthians 15:35-49

Additionally, we are told marvelous things about humanity in Psalm 8 and Psalm 139! We are cared for, we are crowned, we are given dominion and more than all these, we are given the Name of the God who created us and who sustains us that we may praise Him all our days. "I praise you, for I am fearfully and wonderfully made. Wonderful are your works; my soul knows it very well."

26

Isaiah 54:4 "Fear not, for you will not be ashamed."

Read first: Isaiah 54:1-8

The 'you' in this "Fear not!" is Sarah, the wife of Abraham (see Galatians 4) and she is (or she represents) the woman of promise – namely the promise of countless offspring. Since in the time in which Isaiah is preaching God's word Jerusalem is nearly destroyed and the few remaining Jews are in exile, one was likely to wonder if there were any more 'offspring like the sands on the seashore'. Sarah was, and by extension believing Jews were, ashamed and confounded to be found without offspring. But God is the husband. He plants the seed of his word in hearts and makes people children of the promise through faith. God is fathering children, not through biology – as Abraham and Hagar tried to do – but through His promise.

God is declaring his compassion and his restoration after he has shown his 'overflowing anger' – anger which demolished the nation of its citizens. Faithful followers of God need not be feeling 'ashamed', 'confounded', or 'disgraced' because God has only disciplined, not eliminated his people. His covenant of grace is eternal; therefore there will be offspring as promised.

Today, many barren women may be found to pridefully wear the badge of 'Childless'. It is difficult to imagine how such an individual could comprehend the message God is declaring through Isaiah. Multitudes of offspring are marvelous in God's eyes, but barrenness is a blight. God wants a large (enormous) family and he will make sure it happens. Behold, children are a heritage from the LORD, the fruit of the womb a reward. Blessed is the man who fills his quiver with them!

Prayer: Talk with your Father in heaven about your love for families, both biological and spiritual.

> "The Deacon: Let us stand well, let us stand reverently, let us stand in the fear of God, and with compunction of heart. In peace let us pray to the Lord.
> The Priest: For God of peace, mercy, love, compassion, and loving-kindness art Thou, and Thine only-begotten Son, and Thine all-holy Spirit, now and ever.
> The People: Amen.
> The Priest: Peace be to all.
> The People: And to thy spirit."
> – The Divine Liturgy of James

Diving In

"Multitudes of offspring are marvelous in God's eyes, but barrenness is a blight. God wants a large (enormous) family and he will make sure it happens. Behold, children are a heritage from the LORD, the fruit of the womb a reward. Blessed is the man who fills his quiver with them!"

Question:

How does God feel about families with children (biological or adopted)?

1. He commanded it before the Flood: Genesis 1:28

2. He commanded it after the Flood: Genesis 9:1 and 9:7

3. God promised large families: Genesis 17:4, 17:20

4. Large families are blessed and commended: Psalm 127

5. Large families are illustrated in positive terms: Psalm 128

6. Continuing generations are encouraged: Proverbs 17:6

7. Blessing future generations is encouraged: Proverbs 13:22

8. Jesus had quite the large family: Matthew 13:55-56

9. Jesus loved the children: Luke 18:16

10. Jesus is the life: John 14:6 (Those who are in Jesus will express him through working for life and not prohibiting nor ending it.)

Theology

The theology of the family can be expressed very simply: "A man shall leave his father and his mother and cleave to his wife, and they shall become one flesh." Man, woman, children – this is the plan, design and purpose according to the Creator. This is the history of humanity on the planet. And while it will not be the future of humanity in the next life, this fact does not negate, postpone or mitigate the institution of the family while we live on earth.

27

Jeremiah 1:8 "Fear not in the face of them for I am with you to deliver you."

Read first: Jeremiah 1:4-10

"Yea, though I walk through the valley of the shadow of death..." Yes, it is not "if I walk" but "I walk through the valley". Thus young Jeremiah hears from the Lord, "You will be surrounded by evil." And honestly, his tour though darkness will be much of his own doing. Sure, the words of the Lord are the catalyst but it is Jeremiah who will speak them. He gets the oh-so-fun job of breaking down nations and destroying kingdoms. Bad part is he has to do it with words. He can't sit by and send soldiers in, he can't launch missiles from the comfort of an underground bunker. He has to go and see the bad people, tell the bad people they will be destroyed.

This is why few people ever want to be a prophet of God. Ever hear of 'don't shoot the messenger'? In Jeremiah's case they will try to shoot him – guaranteed! Who really wants the job where people either run screaming from you because they know you herald devastation or they run for you to capture you and throw you in a dungeon? But God knows all of this and tells Jeremiah to "Fear Not!" because God will deliver him from the firing squad. This may be somewhat reassuring, but it may not completely salve the reality for Jeremiah that he is the doomsayer.

But perhaps the more interesting question is, "If God formed us in the womb, if God consecrated us – why didn't he do so without fear?" In other words, if God is the builder, why did he include the faulty material of fear? Why not just exclude fear so He wouldn't have to tell us to "Fear not!"? . . . unless fear is necessary to our existence. . . . unless it is not fear which is bad but it is what we fear that makes it unhealthy; an improper use of fear.

Fear is actually a human reality – and not a bad thing at all. We need fear in order to "fear the Lord our God for our good always" (Deuteronomy 6:24 and Jeremiah 32:39). God teaches us how to fear in His word by telling us whom to fear – Him – and who and what not to fear.

Prayer: Talk with your Father in heaven about how you can speak the truth in love.

"When we have come back unto the earnest love of God, He remembers not the former things. God is not as man, for He reproaches us not with the past, neither doth He say, Why wast thou absent so long a time? when we repent; only let us approach Him as we ought. Let us cleave to Him earnestly, and rivet our hearts to His fear."
– John Chrysostom, Homilies on Matthew, LXVII

Diving In

"This is why few people ever want to be a prophet of God. Ever hear of 'don't shoot the messenger'? In Jeremiah's case they will try to shoot him – guaranteed! Who really wants the job where people either run screaming from you because they know you herald devastation or they run for you to capture you and throw you in a dungeon?"

Theology

The Bible records much about the prophets of God; not all pleasant. Read about prophets who:

Didn't want to be a prophet

1. Elijah (wanted to quit): 1 Kings 19
2. Jonah (didn't want the job): Jonah 1
3. Jeremiah (protested his call): Jeremiah 1:6
4. Amos (didn't think he was a prophet. Note – the Hebrew lacks the past tense verb: "I am no prophet, nor am I a prophet's son.") Amos 7:13-15

Were told to do unpleasant things

1. Hosea 1:2-8, 3:1-3
2. Isaiah 20
3. Ezekiel 4:4 - 5: 4
4. Jeremiah 27 and 28
5. 1 Kings 20:35-38

Were killed

1. Zechariah: 2 Chronicles 24:22 (Matthew 23:35)
2. Unnamed: 1 Kings 18:4, 19:10
3. Uriah: Jeremiah 26:20-23
4. Hebrews 11:37 (extra-Biblical record suggests that Isaiah was sawn in two)
5. John the Baptist: Matthew 14:10

28

Jeremiah 10:5 "Fear not them for they cannot do evil."

Read first: Jeremiah 10:1-5

The whole idea of being afraid of stars and comets and cute little figurines made of wood or stone may strike the modern reader as quite silly. But we would do well to remember Herod and Jerusalem: "When Herod the king heard this [the star that heralded the birth of the King], he was troubled, and all Jerusalem with him; and assembling all the chief priests and scribes of the people, he inquired of them where the Christ was to be born." Plus, there are many instances in modern times when sights in the skies have struck fear into the populace. And, in one modern instance with figurines, two self-proclaimed witches performed a public ceremony attempting to curse a Christian American football player – by using a doll/figurine of the athlete. The Christian athlete may not have been afraid, but the witches certainly believed in their evil craft.

These 'signs in the heavens' and 'idols made by craftsmen' are a serious affair. People really do believe this stuff, they really are convinced in their own heart and mind of the 'power' of these things. And very strong personal conviction sways many a person. Events can be suggested to have influence upon other events; outcomes can be persuasively presented as effects of a cause. However, acceptance of such arguments can cloud the facts. Fact number one: the heavens contain signs, not powers. Fact number two: idols are mute, dumb, immobile, lifeless and powerless, a delusion and an illusion. Fact number three: God lives, God is the everlasting king, God is all powerful.

All the necessary arguments on this topic are laid out in Scripture. All the necessary corrections for our misguided attentions are also contained therein. As my father used to say at appropriate times, "Get your head screwed on straight." Indeed. "Thus shall you say to them: 'The gods who did not make the heavens and the earth shall perish from the earth and from under the heavens.'" We do not fear that which perishes but instead Him who is immortal, invisible and all-wise!

Prayer: Talk with your Father in heaven about learning from Him how to refute the foolish and defend the faith, always giving a reason for the hope of a believer.

> "Fear keeps the watch of temporal protection, but knows not how to keep guard permanently."
> – Abmrose, On the Duties of the Clergy, Book II

Diving In

"We do not fear that which perishes but instead Him who is immortal, invisible and all-wise!"

Theology

There is a continual stream of narratives in the Bible which describe the evil actions of men and women. The Bible does not try to hide their actions or minimize the impact of them. Evil is shown to be evil, sin is shown to be sin. The honesty of the Bible about evil is a compelling witness to the Bible's overall truth. Of course the Bible also records the evil actions of otherwise good and Godly people. No one is immune to sinful thoughts and actions.

One common aspect of fear is the fear of the unknown evil. While not asking us to dwell on evil, the Bible clearly reveals the intentions and actions of evil. Perhaps by knowing what evil people are likely to do we may be less afraid of them and more trusting in the God who delivers us from evil. By knowing what evil we might perpetuate, we might flee from temptation and trust God to show us the way out of temptation.

Question

Below is a list of people, both righteous and unrighteous, who did bad things. Identify in a word or two what each one did. Consider if any of their actions are novel or unique; do we still see their evil in our world today?

Bible Reference	Person	Deed	Unique?
Genesis 4	Cain		
Genesis 9:22-24	Ham		
Genesis 38:6-10	Onan		
Joshua 7	Achan		
1 Samuel 28	Saul		
2 Samuel 11	David		
1 Kings 11	Solomon		
1 Kings 21	Jezebel		
2 Kings 5:15-27	Gehazi		
Matthew 2:16-18	Herod		
Matthew 14:1-12	Herod		
Matthew 26:47-55	Judas		
Matthew 26:66-75	Peter		
Acts 5:1-10	Sapphira		
Acts 12:1-5	Herod		

29

Jeremiah 30:10 "Fear not . . . I will save you from far away."

Read first: Jeremiah 30:8-11

This "Fear not!" refers to fearing the possible total annihilation of the Jewish people. This time is so dreadful that even the Lord declares that "there is none like it" and "I will by no means leave you unpunished". So what do we make of this Word of the Lord? He has declared that nearly everyone will die and the rest will be exiled – but "Fear not!" It almost sounds like sarcasm, for who will be left to "Fear not!" if everyone is dead or gone?

Perhaps 'dead and gone' is too strong a statement, however. The presupposition is that everyone will be dead and gone so therefore why waste time speaking to such people. But what if, just possibly, God is trying to keep them in faith until they die; trying to keep them from jumping out of his hands into the fires of everlasting doom when they go off to exile? What if this Word of God is meant to strengthen his people during their last few moments of life on earth? What an odd juxtaposition of actions! God punishes so severely that few will be left alive. God admits that this is necessary because the "hurt is incurable" because their "guilt is great". Yet God wants them to know that He remains merciful, compassionate and faithful to his promises. Is God telling them to "be faithful unto death and I will give you a crown of life"? If so, Wow! How difficult this time must have been and how encouraging this word is meant to be.

Surely God has a vision beyond this life, a vision which sees that this life as it is lived impacts our entrance into the next life. God sees beyond this life, but since He does not (or can not in our sinful condition) open our eyes to the eternal-beyond, he asks that we trust His vision. Faith is the assurance of things hoped for, the conviction of things not seen. This being a true statement, then it takes great faith to "Fear not!" and trust that "I will save you from far away."

As a word from God to a people about to perish, perhaps this word can also give comfort to us when we face the passing of this life and we hope for entrance to the promised Paradise. Our sin is incurable and must die, our guilt is great but it has been forgiven. We "Fear not!" our earthly end for the crown of everlasting life is ours as we are in Jesus Christ.

Prayer: Talk with your Father in heaven about your last days and moments. Ask for a steadfast faith which overcomes during these times.

> "See how Paul has admitted those to be children who are under fear and sins; but has conferred manhood on those who are under faith, by calling them sons, in contradistinction from the children that are under the law: 'For thou art no more a servant,' he says, 'but a son; and if a son, then an heir through God.'"
> – Clement of Alexandria, The Instructor, Book 1

Diving In

"As a word from God to a people about to perish, perhaps this word can also give comfort to us when we face the passing of this life and we hope for entrance to the promised Paradise. Our sin is incurable and must die, our guilt is great but it has been forgiven. We 'Fear not!' our earthly end for the crown of everlasting life is ours as we are in Jesus Christ."

Theology

What is heaven like? This is a good question with many great answers. We are given many verses which tell us what is in heaven. We are told there are angels (numerous passages from Jacob's ladder to the book of Revelation), elders (the book of Revelation) and living creatures (Isaiah, Ezekiel, Revelation). There are horses, trees – cedar, olive, the tree of life – , and the river of the water of life (Psalms, Ezekiel, Revelation). There is a throne, a book, scrolls, trumpets, a city and multitudes of saints (Isaiah, Matthew, Revelation). There are white robes and harps and colored sashes. There is gold galore: bowls, crowns, lamp stands and streets. There is God, the Lamb of God and the Spirit of God. There are rainbows and songs and shouts of praise. And then there is the Bride, the wife of the Lamb, the holy city of Jerusalem: the city's twelve gates are made of single pearls, the walls are jasper and clear as crystal, and the foundation of the city is decorated with jewels of every kind (Zechariah, Revelation).

We are also told what is not in heaven: neither tears, war, death, the enemy and his angels, hunger, poverty, thirst, money, suffering, plagues, nor night. Heaven is, in a word, Paradise, the Paradise of God!

Question

1. How do we live so as to reveal to others that heaven is real? Do we have a faraway look in our eyes? Are we focused on other-worldly things?

2. What love for the things of earth do we have if we live as though they are all going to be destroyed and only heaven will be left?

3. When we help others transition from this life to the next, what comfort of heaven should we give them?

30

Jeremiah 42:11 "Fear not the king of Babylon of whom you are afraid."

Read first: Jeremiah 42:1-22, 43:1-4

God presents an interesting choice, through Jeremiah, to the people of Judah. They can either stay afraid of the king of Babylon now, or they can be really afraid of God later. On the one hand, their fear of the Babylonian army will push them into the wrath of the Lord where they will certainly be afraid and certainly be destroyed. On the other hand, they can stop fearing Babylon now, having real fear about what God will do to them if they join Egypt, and thus avoid God's future wrath. Either way, it comes down to believing God. You can believe God's promises now (about destroying Babylon and destroying you) or you will believe them later (after Babylon and you are both destroyed). Your choice, so to speak, but you will believe God one way or the other.

Rightly placed fear is important to God. He knows his own wrath, his own necessary justice. He also knows his enduring love and mercy. Fearing God, that is 'being afraid of God's wrath', seems to drive a person to the mercies of God where He is ready and willing to embrace you and protect you. Misplaced fear causes you to make poor decisions and keeps you out of a trusting relationship with God.

The people of Judah ended up rejecting the protection of God from earthly foes and so ran smack in to God's wrath. Do we also reject God's protection – both earthly and eternal? Do we trust in "chariots and horses" or do we trust in the name of the Lord our God?

Prayer: Ask your heavenly Father to open your ears to His Word that you might hear both His commands of perfection and His promises of forgiveness.

> "Is it not evident that the Lord Jesus is angry with us when we sin in order that He may convert us through fear of His indignation? His indignation, then, is not the carrying out of vengeance, but rather the working out of forgiveness, for these are His words: 'If thou shalt turn and lament, thou shall be saved.' He waits for our lamentations here, that is, in time, that He may spare us those which shall be eternal. He waits for our tears, that He may pour forth His goodness."
>
> – Ambrose, *Two Books on Repentance*, Book 1

Diving In

"Do we trust in 'chariots and horses' or do we trust in the name of the Lord our God?"

Theology

The great Reformer Martin Luther wrote this on the First Commandment:

> "'You shall have no other gods.' That is: You shall worship me alone as your God. How is this to be understood? What does it mean to have a god? Or, what is God? Answer: A god means that from which we are to expect all good and to which we are to take refuge in all distress, so that to have a God is nothing else than to trust and believe Him from the whole heart. I have often said that the confidence and faith of the heart alone make both God and an idol. If your faith and trust is right, then is your god also true; and, on the other hand, if your trust is false and wrong, then you have not the true God; for these two belong together, faith and God. That upon which you set your heart and put your trust is properly your god."

The Bible speaks a great deal about trust. The book of Psalms has the greatest number of passages on trust. Psalm 56:3-4 has probably the purest and simplest statement on trust: "When I am afraid, I put my trust in you. In God, whose word I praise, in God I trust; I shall not be afraid. What can flesh do to me?"

Question

The Psalms offer perspective on trust from many angles. Trust sometimes involves action, sometimes involves an individual or a group of people, sometimes involves the heart and sometimes is a reaction to outside stimulus. See how trust is illuminated in each of the following verses from Psalms and mediate on what it is to trust in the Lord.

Psalm   Trust . . .

1. 4:5   _____

2. 13:5   _____

3. 20:7   _____

4. 21:7   _____

5. 22:4   _____

6. 22:9   _____

7. 26:1   _____

8. 28:7   _____

9. 37:3   _____

10. 62:8   _____

11. 112:7   _____

12. 118:8   _____

31

Jeremiah 46:27, 28 "Fear not . . . I will save you from far away. . . I am with you."

Read first: Jeremiah 46:25-28

These two "Fear Not!" statements are repetitions from earlier proclamations. Initially, it would seem unimportant to meditate on these because they do not add any new perspectives to understanding all the "Fear not!" statements made by God in the Bible. However, they are significant. Allow me to share a personal story.

When I was in my father's house growing up, he told me nearly every night, and sometimes too many times nearly every night, to "Brush your teeth." Apparently this was something I forgot to do quite regularly. A funny thing happened, however, when as an adult began living in my own home. Every night I would hear his voice tell me, "Brush your teeth." And until I did, I would hear his voice. If I hadn't brushed my teeth I couldn't go to sleep, even, without hearing his voice. His repetition set in concrete the necessity to brush my teeth.

So it is with our Father in heaven's words. Ringing in our ears, how can we forget to "Fear not!" when this matter is so important to our Lord? My earthly father is with me always because his word is with me. My heavenly Father is also with me always because his Word is with me in my mind and heart. The great difference between the two words is that we are responsible for continuing to place our Father in heaven's word in our ears, mind and heart. We are responsible for placing it in the hands, ears, and mouths of our children.

What an excellent way to start and end each and every day – hearing our Lord say, "Fear not for I am with you!" and trusting in these words.

Prayer: Meditate with your Father in heaven on His repeated command to "Fear not!"

> "What? Would you not be afraid of danger in time of persecution, and of losing the most precious Thing you have – Christ? Would you then on this account avoid becoming a Christian? Perish the thought. Such a fear is not for a sane man; such an argument argues insanity."
> – Gregory Nizianzen, Orations, XL

<u>Diving In</u>

"What an excellent way to start and end each and every day – hearing our Lord say, 'Fear not for I am with you!' and trusting in these words."

Theology

> True
> Reliance
> Upon
> Scriptural
> Truth

Question

Proverbs dispenses wisdom often as a comparison or as a contrast. Reflect on these colorful statements of truth and consider how you might incorporate them into your daily conversations.

Proverbs   Compared or Contrasted:

1. 11:28   _____

2. 16:20   _____

3. 28:25   _____

4. 28:26   _____

5. 29:25   _____

6. 31:11   _____

32

Lamentations 3:57 "You came near when I called on you; you said, 'Fear not!'"

Read first: Lamentations 3:52-60

This is a very comforting passage in a book lamenting the destructive wrath of God upon sin and idolatry. Jeremiah is recalling a time when God spoke to him in kind, strengthening words after he called to God in distress. Remembering how God has done the same in our lives brings joy and peace to the heart.

This passage also creates a picture in the mind of a child crying out at night for his daddy. His father comes near and says, "Don't be afraid, I am here." The child is able to relax because his strong and caring father is near. There is no need for the child to fear because he trusts that his daddy will protect him from all harm and danger.

What the child does not know is the fulfillment that his daddy receives from being his child's protector. There is a mutual strengthening that happens, a building up of the relationship between the two people. Perhaps this experience is one way that our Father in heaven teaches earthly fathers the importance of continuing to come to Him for strength and protection. We can only imagine the joy our Father in heaven feels when he is able to come near to us because we have called out. We don't need to imagine our relationship being stronger – of that we are blessed to know in our heart.

Prayer: Speak with your Father in heaven about strengthening your relationship with Him.

> "The demons, therefore, if they see all Christians, and monks especially, labouring cheerfully and advancing, first make an attack by temptation and place hindrances to hamper our way, to wit, evil thoughts. But we need not fear their suggestions, for by prayer, fasting, and faith in the Lord their attack immediately fails. But even when it does they cease not, but knavishly by subtlety come on again. For when they cannot deceive the heart openly with foul pleasures they approach in different guise, and thenceforth shaping displays they attempt to strike fear, changing their shapes, taking the forms of women, wild beasts, creeping things, gigantic bodies, and troops of soldiers. But not even then need ye fear their deceitful displays. For they are nothing and quickly disappear, especially if a man fortify himself beforehand with faith and the sign of the cross."
> – Athanasius, Life of Antony

Diving In

"There is no need for the child to fear because he trusts that his daddy will protect him from all harm and danger."

Theology

While the Bible makes clear repeatedly that we are to trust in God, it also describes the things which people tend to trust in instead of God. As the Reformer Martin Luther wrote, "To have a God is nothing else than to trust and believe Him from the whole heart. I have often said that the confidence and faith of the heart alone make both God and an idol."

Question

Jeremiah compiles probably the most comprehensive list of things we should not trust in. Reflect upon what he identifies and repent and seek the Lord's forgiveness for times you have trusted in these things above Him.

      Jeremiah   Trust not in . . .

1. 9:4 _____

2. 12:5 _____

3. 13:25 _____

4. 17:5 _____

5. 48:7 _____

6. 49:4 _____

33

Ezekiel 2:6 "Fear not them . . . nor their words."

Read first: Ezekiel 2:1-7

This reading is collection of very sad truths and very unpleasant predictions. Certainly God tells Ezekiel to "Fear not!" but the joy of this word is pretty much sucked out when it is followed by "you will sit on scorpions" and "you will have briers and thorns with you". And then there is the part about. "I've called you to be a prophet, your life will now be a miserable set of constant conflicts."

Ezekiel is basically going to war, with and for God, against God's people. The opponent in this war is described as the 'rebellious house' and the owner of the house is really, really upset. Normally we tell our children not to call people names but here God doesn't hold back on the truth and calls His people impudent, stubborn, and rebels. Ezekiel is sent to these not-so-fine folks to tell them what they don't want to hear, won't like hearing, and will ultimately refuse to hear. Perhaps this "Fear not!" isn't supposed to comfort Ezekiel as much as it is to preempt any discussion on Ezekiel's part about how he feels in all this. God's great passion on this matter overrides all concerns the newly appointed prophet might have.

God's call to serve Him can often be like this. He chooses and we go, our complaints and reasons and uneasiness not withstanding. God tells us where to go, sometimes tells us what to do and always promises His presence. He does not often promise success, however. In Ezekiel's case God promises the opposite – failure. And he promises trouble and suffering. In the battle of words between God and Israel, Ezekiel is caught, or placed, in the middle. On the one hand the rebels will see no point in threatening God so they will threaten Ezekiel. On the other hand, Ezekiel shouts irreversible and irrevocable promises of destruction and death to people who are actually his kinsmen. Being a prophet of God was no joyous experience at this time in Israel's history.

Still, the word is there. "Fear not!" And this word is greater than all the world. "I sought the LORD, and he answered me and delivered me from all my fears. Those who look to him are radiant, and their faces shall never be ashamed. This poor man cried, and the LORD heard him and saved him out of all his troubles. The angel of the LORD encamps around those who fear him, and delivers them."

Prayer: Talk with your Father in heaven about whether the conflicts around you are your own doing or the place where God calling is you to witness. Repent if you are the cause of sinful conflict; ask for boldness if this is your time to witness.

Diving In

"Still, the word is there. 'Fear not!' And this word is greater than all the world."

Theology

In an attempt to define reality, some people believe that reality is what a person can experience, touch, taste, feel, etc. Other people believe that reality cannot be defined as a there are possible realities beyond our ability to sense them, realities which include intuition and alternate dimensions.

The Bible demonstrates that it is the Word of God which creates and defines reality. Without the Word, there would not be anything: "without him was not any thing made that was made. . . " John 1:3. The Word of God has also made things both visible and invisible to humans: "For by him all things were created, in heaven and on earth, visible and invisible, whether thrones or dominions or rulers or authorities – all things were created through him and for him." Colossians 1:16.

Question

The following passages show how the Word of God creates realities which we can and cannot see. What other passages of Scripture show God creating reality through his spoken word?

1. Genesis 1 Each time God spoke, things came into existence.

2. Genesis 2 Before God said that Adam could die, there was no death.

3. Mark 1:41 Jesus spoke and the leper really was clean.

4. Mark 2:5 Jesus spoke a reality (forgiveness) which could not be seen.

5. Mark 2:12 Jesus spoke a reality (healing) which could be seen.

6. John 19:30   Jesus spoke a reality which eliminated other possibilities.

7. Isaiah 43:1   God creates identity and ownership

8. Luke 22:19   Jesus creates a reality beyond physical sensation.

34

Ezekiel 3:9 "Fear them not, nor be dismayed at their looks."

Read first: Ezekiel 3:4-11

This lively passage about the faces and foreheads of Ezekiel and the Israelites is quite unique in the Bible. God describes the hard foreheads and stubborn hearts of the people and then he tells Ezekiel that He has given Ezekiel just as hard a head and just as stubborn a disposition as they have. It is as if God is setting up two battering rams and letting them go at each other.

However, the English translators stumble on how to render a word in verse 9. One Bible uses 'adamant', another uses 'emery', another avoids it all together. The Hebrew word refers to a substance impenetrably hard and unyielding. It is suggested that this may be a diamond of some sort, or at least what would come to mind when we think 'diamond'. If we honestly translate this Hebrew word we see that God has made his battering ram just a bit more tough than the Israelite ram. Sure, both are unrelenting, but God's ram has this horn, as it were, made of an unbreakable substance. If we imagine these two rams butting heads, we can see that God's ram is likely to not just stop the other in its tracks but actually shatter it. With this ram in mind, God says to Ezekiel, "Fear them not, nor their looks!"

What a fascinating detail! God wants Ezekiel to go face to face (battering ram to battering ram) with them and he doesn't want Ezekiel to blink, shrink, feint, or flinch. It is natural to fear the collision with something hard and inflexible; it makes a person cringe just before impact. But God wants the unnatural, or maybe better said the supernatural, to be on display.

This "Fear not!" brings to mind this word of Jesus: "When they deliver you over, do not be anxious how you are to speak or what you are to say, for what you are to say will be given to you in that hour. For it is not you who speak, but the Spirit of your Father speaking through you." And whatever the Spirit speaks is sure to split the enemy into pieces!

Prayer: Talk with your Father in heaven about hiding His Word in your heart so you may have the right words to speak when you are 'delivered over'.

> "If you have not faith, do not fear beasts so much as your faithlessness, which renders you susceptible of all corruption."
> – Basil, Homily IX

Diving In

"This 'Fear not!' brings to mind this word of Jesus: 'When they deliver you over, do not be anxious how you are to speak or what you are to say, for what you are to say will be given to you in that hour.'"

Theology

The Word of God is illustrated in a number of different ways, offering us dynamic visual images to mediate upon. In fact, much of the Bible communicates meaning through symbols, stories, parables, pictures, metaphors and similes. The layers of meaning in these literary forms help us to establish a firm physical and spiritual connection to the ideas and truths of God.

A casual reading of the Bible spurs the mind to imagine the scene of many dramatic events or to explore the depth of imagery conveyed through poem and parable. But this level of reading produces a superficial (yet still beneficial) understanding. The next steps after studying the Scriptures for information and learning is to meditate upon the teachings of God and then fearfully implement God's truth in our lives.

Question

The following are a selection of Scripture passages which illustrate the Word of God using comparison or metaphor. In some cases the Word will break and destroy, in others it will grow and sustain. Consider what each illustration means for your life.

Scripture passage	The Word of God is . . .	What this means it will do in my life . . .
Jeremiah 23:29a	like fire	
Jeremiah 23:29b		
Psalm 119:105a		
Psalm 119:105b		
Matthew 4:4		
Luke 8:11		
Hebrews 4:12		
James 1:22-25		

35

Daniel 10:12 "Fear not . . . your words have been heard."

Read first: Daniel 10:2-12

The appearance / vision / visitation of the heavenly being knocks Daniel off his feet, literally. Daniel is truly a humble servant of the Lord, aware of his sinfulness and of the sinfulness of his people and when faced with the holy representative of the Almighty God he can do only one thing: tremble. Daniel's companions tremble as well in verse 7, Daniel shakes in verse 10, and he quakes in verse 11.

Daniel's fear is physical. He loses his strength, his balance, his breath. Daniel's fear comes as the result of the visitor's frightening visage and connection to the almighty source of power. Daniel gets 'weak in the knees' and gets 'cotton mouth' because of the unveiled greatness of this "man clothed in linen".

This is one of the Biblical moments which we often both wish would happen to us and wish would never happen to us. To see beyond the veil of this existence holds such excitement; the glory of heaven and of the angels and of the presence of God. Yet such a vision holds such holy power that we could not help but be crushed, wiped away, and annihilated by even the briefest of glimpses.

To hear, "Fear not!" when seeing an angel means that the person is both privileged to survive the encounter and burdened with its memory. Daniel says of one vision, "As for me, Daniel, my thoughts greatly alarmed me, and my color changed, but I kept the matter in my heart." and of another, "And I, Daniel, was overcome and lay sick for some days. Then I rose and went about the king's business, but I was appalled by the vision and did not understand it."

The sweetest part of this message from God through the angel, however, are the words "Your words have been heard." God does listen and we should draw comfort and strength from this reality.

Prayer: Thank your heavenly Father that he listens to you – and always has.

> "Come let us compare the king and the prisoner, and thou wilt often see the latter in pleasure and sporting and leaping, while the former with his diadem and purple robe is in despair, and hath innumerable cares, and is dead with fear."
> – John Chrysostom, Homilies on Matthew, LIII

Diving In

"The sweetest part of this message from God through the angel, however, are the words 'Your words have been heard.' God does listen and we should draw comfort and strength from this reality."

Theology

God is Spirit. This is what Jesus teaches in John 4:24 to the woman from Samaria. Yet, God hears. How can a spiritual being hear? The answer to this is probably beyond our human understanding because we are mortal and physically bound and as such cannot fully comprehend the realities of the spiritual world.

To bridge the gap in our understanding and to help strengthen our relationship with our Spirit-God, God uses language which describes his actions and attributes in human terms. For instance, God is said to have a mind and a memory (Numbers 23:19 and Genesis 9:16) and strong feelings (Exodus 20:5 and Judges 2:18). The formal term for this is 'anthropomorphism' which is two Greek words; anthropos, meaning man, and morphe, meaning form.

Question

What other anthropomorphisms does the Bible use to describe God? What is God communicating through each of these body parts – what does He want his children to understand about how he relates to us? How might God be teaching one dimension of 'created in His image'?

1. Exodus 3:20, 33:22, Isaiah 10:13

2. Numbers 6:25, Psalm 80:3

3. Genesis 2:7, Psalm 33:6, Job 33:4

4. Psalm 34:15a, Proverbs 15:3, 2 Chronicles 16:9, Hebrews 4:13

5. Psalm 34:15b, 1 Samuel 8:21, Psalm 86

6. Deuteronomy 7:19, Psalm 136:12, Jeremiah 27:5

7. Exodus 24:10, Isaiah 66:1, Psalm 18:9

36

Daniel 10:19 "Fear not, peace be with you."

Read first: Daniel 10:13-21

A more literal translation of verses 18 and 19 is helpful.

> "Again, the appearing-to-be-a-man touched me and strengthened me. And he said, 'O desired/coveted man, fear not, peace to you, be strong and strong.'"

It's not as smooth as you will find in the English Bibles, but it is more accurate. And this literal translation reveals some interesting things. First, Daniel continues to relate that his visitor appears to be a man. He's not really a man but he sort of looks like one. So Daniel is confused by what he sees and by how to identify it. The sort-of-man also calls Daniel by a descriptor difficult to put into English. The word isn't really about love; it is about desire, lust, coveting. What does that mean? Well, it can mean either that the enemy wants Daniel or that Daniel is desired for his faith and/or Godly lifestyle. Either way, it's a nice compliment that may foreshadow Mary's compliment in Luke 1:28, "Greetings, O Favored One". Finally, the phrase, "be strong and strong" while strange in English may have held a meaning similar to 'stand up on your feet' (what else are you going to stand on?) or 'sit up and get your back straight' (obviously if one sits up, their back will be straight).

In the midst of this section is the "Fear not!" phrase paired nicely with "Shalom". The angel apparently sees Daniel's confusion and his sudden physical weakness and attempts to comfort Daniel by saying that while his very presence is driving Daniel's mind and body to mush, there is no need to be afraid; he – the visitor – is not here to hurt Daniel. The grouping of fear and peace is noteworthy as well. This is the second time, and likely only other time, in the Bible where these two are paired. Gideon is told in Judges 6, "Peace to you. Fear not! You will not die."

Our weakness and frailty is never so evident as it is in the presence of God – or his holy representatives. In this case the opposite of fear appears to be peace, not so much trust. Perhaps trust comes when we cannot see God, and peace when we can.

Prayer: Talk with your Father in heaven about the peace that passes understanding, about peace with Him through his Son, about the word of peace which has been given to you to give to others.

Diving In

"Perhaps trust comes when we cannot see God, and peace when we can."

Theology

Blindness. From the blindness with which the angels struck Sodom to Jesus calling the members of the church in Laodicea blind, this affliction runs through the entire Bible. Some blindness is physical, like the blind man in John 9, some is metaphorical, like the unbelievers in 2 Corinthians 4. Some blindness is cured, as in the case of the man in Mark 8, some blindness is inflicted as in Isaiah 6 or 2 Kings 6. In every instance, blindness is the undesired condition.

There are also instances where temporary blindness was given to men, and later lifted, as on the road to Emmaus in Luke 24 and when Saul was visited by Jesus on the road to Damascus in Acts 13. There are still other instances where blindness was given as a punishment (Judges 16:21 and 2 Kings 25:7). And blindness as a result of old age is recorded to have happened to Isaac, Jacob, Eli and Ahijah.

Yet, the Bible also teaches that blindness is a work of God. Moses is told by God in Exodus 4:11, "Who has made man's mouth? Who makes him mute, or deaf, or seeing, or blind? Is it not I, the LORD?" Jesus later answers the disciples' question, "Rabbi, who sinned, this man or his parents, that he was born blind?" with these words, "It was not that this man sinned, or his parents, but that the works of God might be displayed in him."

When it comes to faith, not being able to see is implicitly contrasted with simply not seeing. Faith is a trust in the unseen; it is a firm conviction that there is something to see but seeing whatever it is holds a lesser value than trusting that it is there. Faith is, as the Reformers boldly proclaimed, "the firm acceptance of God's offer promising forgiveness of sins and justification."

Questions

How does the Bible describe the 'blindness' of faith?

1. Hebrews 11:1 _____

2. Romans 8:24 _____

3. 1 Peter 1:8 _____

4. John 20:29 _____

5. 2 Corinthians 5:7 _____

37

Hosea 10:3 "We fear not the Lord."

Read first: Hosea 10:1-4

This is an interesting twist of the "Fear not!" phrase. It is God who places these words in the mouth of his people when he predicts that they will be bitter because their king has been taken away. God anticipates an insolent attitude which says, "God gave us a king because he said we did not fear him. Now he's taken that king away from us so that we would see that the king could do nothing for us. Even if we had a king now, what good would it do? Either way we lose. Woe to us! God thinks we hate him and now he's going to let us have it."

As unpleasant as this prophetic word sounds, there is much to be said about its accuracy. Even though God warned against it, there continued to be despondency, idolatry, and despair among God's people. They simply did not fear God. Perhaps they had forgotten how to fear God; surely many nations in history have experienced such a crisis. God wanted the people to fear him, in both the sense of respect of His holiness and the sense of terror over his judgment, but they would do neither.

So here is a case where lack of fear is the problem. Most often the "Fear Not!" phrase has been spoken to counter unnecessary fear; sometimes it has been to counter misplaced fear. Now there is a stony-hearted listlessness toward God. What do you do with such people? Start over?

Well, that is pretty much what God did. He started over with a remnant which He hoped would fear him. And for a while they did. . . but then things went down again. So God started a new covenant which was both the old covenant made new and better and a new people grafted into the old stock. Will the people of this new covenant continue to fear the Lord? Let us all work to see this reality in our lifetime!

Prayer: Talk with your Father in heaven about the lack of fear in your nation.

> "For many fear adverse circumstances, fear not prosperous circumstances. Prosperity is more perilous to soul than adversity to body. First, prosperity doth corrupt, in order that adversity may find something to break. My brethren, stricter watch must be kept against felicity."
> – Augustine, Expositions on the Psalms, Psalm 51

Diving In

"Now there is a stony-hearted listlessness toward God. What do you do with such people? Start over?"

Theology

Children often proclaim a 'do over' when they are playing and innocent mistakes are made or when circumstances out of their control cause a stoppage of play. God declared several 'do over's' in the Bible, but none of them came as a result of innocent mistakes or circumstances out of His control. Rather, sin was so bad that God needed to set things back on track. Significantly, God's 'do over' system followed the same pattern of one (or few) to many and back again. In His infinite patience, and with his command and provision to be fruitful and multiply, God could 'do over' as many times as he wanted, but He was always moving history forward to its ultimate conclusion.

Question

What were God's great 'Do Over's'? Are there other similar events in history after the days recorded in the New Testament? Use the chart below to help guide your reflections.

Bible story	Notes/Reflections	Commentary
The Flood, Genesis 6-9		God started over with just eight people.
The Wilderness, Numbers 14, 20-38, Hebrews 3:7-19		God started over after everyone over the age of 20 had died.
Remnant Returns, Isaiah 10:20-27, Nehemiah, Ezra		God started over by bringing back to Jerusalem after 70 years just some Israelites.
Disciples of Jesus, Matthew 28:19-20, Mark, 16:19-20, Acts 1-2		Jesus started over (or started the new covenant) with 12 men and many others who followed their leadership and example.

38

Joel 2:21 "Fear not, O land."

Read first: Joel 2:18-27

What joy there is when God speaks directly to his creation! The land, seas, mountains, valleys, stars, all of it is significant and precious to Him. These all declare the wonder and glory of God. This speaks loudly and clearly about how we too should regard these things.

Here through the prophet Joel God is telling the land to "Fear not!" because the hardship it is under will soon end. In chapter 1 we are reminded that fields have been destroyed and that wine and oil are gone; the ground mourns because the trees of the field are dried up. Early in chapter 2 we are reminded of earthquakes, darkened moon, stars and sun.

But "Fear not!" because the Lord will restore what has been lost, rains will come again, pastures will green, trees will bear fruit and oil and wine will be found in abundance. Creation, as the apostle Paul teaches, groans in its bondage to corruption but this is not an everlasting condition. No! It is temporary and freedom will come. There is the new earth which Isaiah speaks about (chapters 65 and 66) and John too (Revelation 21).

Does this mean the trees and the grass and the pea plants are alive? No, hardly. But we should take Jesus literally when he says that the rocks can cry out praises to God. They may not sprout forth a mouth and vocal cords but all which God has called into existence fundamentally resounds with His creative power and shows forth his design and purpose. Whatever the form of praise which the elements and the atoms and the molecules are capable of it is surely divine in origin and will be marvelous to behold.

The bottom line is this: God cares not just for the people who live on the land, but for the created land itself. All should "Fear not!" and all should "Praise the Lord!"

Prayer: Talk with your Father in heaven about following His direction in having dominion over the earth.

> "Oftentimes doubt wearies the mind more where the fear of danger is strong; and it is more burdensome to fear lest something should happen than to bear what one already knows has happened. For the one increases the amount of fear, the other looks forward to the end of its grief."
> – Ambrose, On the Decease of Saytrus, Book II

Diving In

"What joy there is when God speaks directly to his creation! The land, seas, mountains, valleys, stars, all of it is as real and as precious to Him as anything else. This speaks loudly and clearly about how we too should regard these things."

Theology

Where creation came from and how it is to be regarded is not an open question in Scripture. Looking at stars in specific, we learn that stars were created on the fourth day:

> "And God said, 'Let there be lights in the expanse of the heavens to separate the day from the night. And let them be for signs and for seasons, and for days and years, and let them be lights in the expanse of the heavens to give light upon the earth.' And it was so. And God made the two great lights—the greater light to rule the day and the lesser light to rule the night—and the stars." (Genesis 1:14-16)

Stars, as a created thing, are to be appreciated, followed, but never worshiped:

> "You shall not make for yourself a carved image, or any likeness of anything that is in heaven above . . . . You shall not bow down to them or serve them, for I the LORD your God am a jealous God." (Exodus 20:4-5)

Question

Stars are found throughout Scripture. Study the following passages to learn more about stars and how God has purpose for them.

1. Genesis 15:5 and Deuteronomy 1:10 _____

2. Psalm 8:3 and 147:4 _____

3. Isaiah 47:13 and Amos 5:26 _____

4. Jeremiah 31:35 and Matthew 2:9 _____

5. Isaiah 13:10 and Luke 21:25 _____

39

Joel 2:22 "Fear not, you beasts of the field."

Read first: Joel 2:18-27

After carefully reading the book of Jonah, it is easy to have a great appreciation for animals. But not because of the fish which swallowed the prophet. No, it is the less noteworthy animals in Jonah which teach us. Do you remember those? The cattle, the herds, and the flocks?!

The herds and flocks show up in chapter 3 when the king of Nineveh withholds from them food and water and then commands that they be covered with the itchy-scratchy sackcloth of mourning. Then God makes a most remarkable statement which ends the book, "And should not I pity Nineveh, that great city, in which there are more than 120,000 persons who do not know their right hand from their left, *and also much cattle?*" Wow! The cattle matter!

As with the land in chapter 1, Joel reminds us that the beasts of the field suffer too. "How the beasts groan! The herds of cattle are perplexed because there is no pasture for them; even the flocks of sheep suffer." And to these simple and mute creatures God speaks to tell them to "Fear not!" The pastures will be green and grazing and space will be abundant.

Amazingly, there is nothing in all of creation which God does not seek to reassure with his call to fearless living. The land, the animals, the people – all these are at some time frightened and in need of God's redirection and security. Surely if a cow can heed the word of God to "Fear not!" so too can we.

Prayer: Ask your Father in heaven to renew your wonder and appreciation for the animals of the earth.

> "The soul can with difficulty be recalled to those good things from which it has fallen, and is with difficulty dragged away from those evils to which it has become accustomed. If at any time thou showest a disposition to blame thyself, then perhaps, through the medicine of repentance, I should cherish good hopes regarding thee. But when thou altogether despisest fear, and rejectest with scorn the very faith of Christ, it were better for thee that thou hadst never been born from the womb."
> – John of Damascus. Fragments of Justin Martyr

Diving In

"The herds and flocks show up in chapter 3 when the king of Nineveh withholds from them food and water and then commands that they be covered with the itchy-scratchy sackcloth of mourning."

Theology

A practice long since departed from the western world, the wearing of sackcloth was a visual and physical reminder of mourning, repentance, and sometimes woe. Not only did sackcloth indicate to others the mental, spiritual and emotional state of the wearer, it caused great skin irritation to the person clothed in it – both during and afterwards. Because of the significant experience that sackcloth provided it became a figurative expression of great sadness as well.

Question

A variety of people wore sackcloth in the Bible. Collect the list and study it for the number of times people of prominence, verses common folk, put on this symbol of mourning and repentance.

Bible Verse	Person	Reason for sackcloth	Person's position or rank
Genesis 37:34	Jacob	Death of Joseph	Head of family and tribe
2 Samuel 3:31			
1 Kings 21:27			
2 Kings 6:30			
2 Kings 19:1			
Esther 4:1			
Joel 1:13			
Jonah 3:6			
Revelation 11:3			

40

Zephaniah 3:16 "On that day it shall be said to Jerusalem, 'Fear not!'"

Read first: Zephaniah 3:14-17

This "Fear not!" proclaims the abundant joy of God in a number of ways. First, the judgments of the Lord are taken away – there is no need to fear his wrath anymore. Second, the Lord is in the midst of the people – there is no need to fear that he has left or will ever leave again. Third, since the Lord is present evil is not – there is no king, nation, or person to be afraid of again. Fourth, and most precious, the Lord will rejoice over you, he will love you, he will exult over you with singing.

To imagine God rejoicing over us, coming near to our heart with his love and singing about us may seem a bit excessive. But God is passionately in love with his people! In return, how can we help but be passionately in love with Him?! When our God is present there is no fear. Each of us can call out to another, "Fear not!" and we can laugh at the idea of ever having been afraid.

This day described in Zephaniah is still a day to come, but we can anticipate its arrival and practice its exultant and exuberant lifestyle. We can continue to fall in love with our Lord. We can sing loudly about and to our Lord, we can rejoice with gladness that we have been saved and called to proclaim the good news that God wants all to be saved through his son Jesus.

Prayer: Ask your Father in heaven to renew your joy in Him.

> "Now that is the will of God which Christ both did and taught. Humility in conversation; steadfastness in faith; modesty in words; justice in deeds; mercifulness in works; discipline in morals; to be unable to do a wrong, and to be able to bear a wrong when done; to keep peace with the brethren; to love God with all one's heart; to love Him in that He is a Father; to fear Him in that He is God; to prefer nothing whatever to Christ, because He did not prefer anything to us; to adhere inseparably to His love; to stand by His cross bravely and faithfully; when there is any contest on behalf of His name and honour, to exhibit in discourse that constancy wherewith we make confession; in torture, that confidence wherewith we do battle; in death, that patience whereby we are crowned;-this is to desire to be fellow-heirs with Christ; this is to do the commandment of God; this is to fulfil the will of the Father."
> – Cyprian, Treatise IV

Diving In

"Fourth, and most precious, the Lord will rejoice over you, he will love you, he will exult over you with singing."

Theology

Lots of people are embarrassed to sing a solo in public but very happy to sing in private or with a large group of other singers. Folks who simply do not like to sing nevertheless enjoy music and song and could not imagine life without it. Fundamentally, our song and our enjoyment of song comes as a result of being created in the image of God. The Scriptures are full of singing and songs and Zephaniah 3 records the most amazing statement about God himself singing. Hebrews 2 cites Psalm 22 and teaches us that Jesus also sings in praise to His Father.

Question

A thorough study of singing in the Bible is a rewarding and uplifting project. Below is a framework to help you begin.

- Singing began (Job 38:7), was developed by (Genesis 4:21) and continues in (Revelation 5:9 and 15:3).
- Composition is defined as needing to be (Psalm 33:33 and Isaiah 42:10).
- Music involves not only the voice but (Psalm 144:9 and 150:4 and Revelation 15:2).
- Great men have written songs (Exodus 51 and 2 Samuel 22 and 1 Kings 4:32).
- Corporate worship and singing are connected (1 Chronicles 25, Ezra 2:64-70).

- Strong emotions and songs work in tandem (Psalm 28:7, 42:4, Jeremiah 30:19, Ephesians 5:19 as well as 2 Samuel, 2 Chronicles 35:25).
- The content of worship songs should focus upon (Psalm 59:16, 101:1, 119:172, 138:5).

Consider now the following:

- Do the songs you sing fit in the Biblical framework?
- What does God expect from your song?

41

Haggai 2:5 "My Spirit remains among you. Fear not!"

Read first: Haggai 2:1-9

This "Fear not!" addresses the concern of being dedicated to and generous toward the house of God. God's people have returned from exile and have been living in, apparently, posh homes while the temple lies in ruins. In response to this lack of devotion, God has withheld rain in the hopes of getting every one's attention. The prophet Haggai is sent to tell the political leader, the religious leader and the people to do the work of rebuilding and outfitting God's house. They are to "Fear Not!" because God's Spirit is among them and God will bring to ruin the other nations which will result in wealth being poured into God's house.

The thought of being afraid to work on the Lord's house is an interesting departure from most, if not all, of the previous instances of fear. Maybe the people were afraid that their work would be for nothing, that either some other nation would come to destroy it or that once they got it complete it would be an empty shell like an abandoned barn or storage shed. In any event God promises that the strength of the people would not go unrewarded. Just the opposite – God was going to bring the "treasures of all nations" and make this house "greater than the former."

Again, God's presence is the foundation for fearless living and specifically in this case the reason the people should fearlessly work. We may learn two lessons from this "Fear not!" First, God cares about his place of worship, the place where His people gather to pray and praise. Second, God cares about us, about how we desire to do work which has purpose and meaning. We are created to work, as God testifies in the Bible's first book, and he will ensure such work is worthwhile.

Prayer: Talk with your Father in heaven about the opportunities to work which He has set before you and equipped you to accomplish.

> "For no one can feel confident regarding a good which he knows can be taken from him, although he wishes to keep and cherish it. But if a man feels no confidence regarding the good which he enjoys, how can he be happy while in such fear of losing it?"
> – Augustine, On the Morals of the Church

Diving In

"They are to 'Fear Not!' because God's Spirit is among them."

Theology

In the Old Testament, the third person of the Trinity is often referred to as the "Spirit" or the "Spirit of God" whereas in the New Testament, he is most often called the "Holy Spirit". Sometimes the word spirit is meant to refer to a person's soul (Numbers 27:16) or personality (Numbers 5:14), liveliness or will to live (Joshua 2:11) or abilities (Exodus 28:3). One of the most striking aspects to the Spirit's existence is that He is always in motion, either filling or coming upon or leaving or being poured out.

Question

Study the following and consider how the Spirit's movement helps you know Him and see Him work. Ponder also C.S. Lewis' related insight: "I believe in Christianity as I believe that the sun has risen: not only because I see it, but because by it I see everything else."

Bible Verse	Spirit's movement	Resulting Evidence
Genesis 1:2	hovering	creation
Exodus 31:3		
Numbers 11:17		
Judges 14:6		
1 Samuel 10:6		

Bible Verse	Spirit's movement	Resulting Evidence
Psalm 104:30		
Isaiah 59:21		
Ezekiel 3		
Matthew 3:16		
Mark 1:12		
Luke 1:35		
Luke 4:18		
John 16:13		
Acts 2:4		
Acts 13:9		
Romans 1:14		
1 Corinthians 3:16		
Titus 3:5		
Revelation 2:7		

42

Zechariah 8:13, 15 "Fear not!"

Read first: Zechariah 8:9-17

It is poignant that the last "Fear not!" in the Old Testament would be the one where God says, "I will not deal with you as I did your fathers; I purpose good, peace, blessing, salvation." This is the word which shines the great light of hope upon the One to come who brought good, peace, blessing and salvation to all children of the promise, children not by blood but by faith.

God's people were afraid of him, and rightly so given the enormity of the wrath they endured as a result of their rebellion and sin. They were probably fully aware of their own inherent failings which would bring them right back to the same place their fathers found themselves – right smack in the cross-hairs of God's righteous anger. They were afraid of God because they knew they could not become righteous nor survive God's righteousness.

But God promises a different solution this time. His wrath would instead be placed upon One who could bear the great burden. In turn the people would be passed over and peace and life would be theirs, and theirs in abundance.

This interpretation, of course, comes from reading history back into the promise. We know that God's chosen Israel descended once again into rebellion and God's permission was given to the Roman nation to scatter them once again to the corners of the earth. Different this time was the Peace which was bought to the city of Jerusalem before that brutal scattering and different was that this Peace went scattered to the world as well, not in punishment but in a sowing of love, forgiveness, and gospel proclamation. Now we await the complete fulfilling of the promise, where all will stream to the city of God to "seek the Lord of hosts". And without a doubt they will make this journey fearing only one thing – the Lord their God.

Prayer: Talk with your Father in heaven about your role in the Gospel proclamation to the world.

> "His body was now all but cold, and nought was left of life but reason. Yet with eyes wide open he kept repeating, 'Go forth, what do you fear? Go forth, my soul, why do you hesitate? You have served Christ nearly seventy years, and do you fear death?' Thus saying he breathed his last."
> – Jerome, The Life of Hilarion

Diving In

"This is the word which shines the great light of hope upon the One to come who brought good, peace, blessing and salvation to all children of the promise, children not by blood but by faith."

Question

What is the likelihood that a Jewish man in Palestine in the first century would be able to fulfill all of these prophesies about the Messiah?

The Messiah was to . . .

1. Be born in _____ (Micah 5:2)

and

2. Be a descendant of _____ (Jeremiah 23:5)

and

3. Would leave the nation of _____ (Hosea 11:1)

and

4. Be preceded by _____ (Isaiah 40:3)

and

5. Heal the _____ (Isaiah 29:18)

and

6. Be a light to _____ (Isaiah 49:6)

and

7. Be betrayed for _____ (Zechariah 11:13)

and

8. During his trial be _____ (Isaiah 53:7)

and

9. Be _____ in hands and feet (Psalm 22:16)

and

10. Have his clothing _____ (Psalm 22:18)

and

11. Be buried in _____ (Isaiah 53:9)

and later,

12. Have his followers _____ (Zechariah 12:7)?

Theology

These prophesies and many, many more are a testimony to the integrity of the Scriptures centered in Jesus Christ and an unmistakable sign that Jesus of Nazareth is exactly whom he claimed to be. The likelihood, or the odds, that a Jewish man in Palestine in the first century would be able to fulfill even just these twelve predictions made hundreds of years before his birth, is so enormous that the only conclusion a sane person can reach is that Jesus is the Christ, the Son of God. The only question which remains is whether this sane person will accept the forgiveness offered in the blood of Jesus or reject it.

The question of who Jesus of Nazareth is has been examined and debated for generations and each one concludes the same: Jesus is who he said he was. The difficult question is not fact but faith. This is the sum and the point of Christian evangelism and apologetic work – to present, without fear, the person of Jesus Christ as living, died and living again for the salvation of the world.

The Bible study lessons for the New Testament occurrences of the phrase, "Fear Not!" depart from the style used previously and instead focus on some of the major characters in the New Testament history. In each lesson, there is an overview of a person or persons. Next there are three questions for consideration and meditation which help you to discover in yourself elements of similarity and dissimilarity with the character being studied. Sometimes you may find that your fears and their fears are similar; perhaps your sins and theirs are similar. You may find that your vocational needs do not mesh with the character but nevertheless their story gives you insight into a friend or neighbor's fears, efforts and needs. I hope that you will be blessed as you contemplate the significance of God's "Fear Not!" word in each of their lives, your life, and the lives of future believers in the Lord Jesus.

43

Matthew 1:20 "Fear not to take Mary as your wife."

Read first: Matthew 1:18-25

This is the first "Fear not!" in the New Testament. Many have heard this verse their entire life. But it is in this study that we find new meaning perhaps, and certainly blessed assurance.

God comes to Joseph because he has decided to divorce Mary. Joseph is described as being unwilling to put Mary to shame; even in divorce. But what does that mean? If we consider Deuteronomy 24, Joseph wants to divorce Mary secretly, essentially (which is the sense of the Greek here). If no one finds out that she was divorced, maybe she can marry the 'other man'. See, it is this unknown 'other man' who is in the picture here rivaling Joseph's immense love for Mary.

Mary has no doubt told Joseph the truth but he cannot accept it. He can accept what he sees and knows, that Mary is with child and it is not his. Yet his love for this young woman is not diminished; he desires to protect her, even in this moment of apparent infidelity. But a mother raising God's son alone is not

God's plan so God comes to Joseph and tells him to "Fear not!" "Fear not!" what? Do not fear that Mary does not love you. Do not fear the possibility that she has been unfaithful. Indeed it is just the opposite – Mary loves Joseph and Mary is faithful and it is in this family relationship that God desires his son to be raised.

God is not only looking out for his son, but caring for the heart of Joseph. Like a similar case about two thousand years before, when God told a father to "Fear not!" to go down to Egypt and be with his son (also named Joseph), God tells this man that love is not forgotten, forgiveness is free, and the future is in God's mighty hands. God knows the quiet fears of our hearts and moves, as a gracious and loving Father, to comfort us.

Prayer: Talk with your Father in heaven about the level of trust you have in your relationships.

> "Let us continue therefore in the fear of God's name: the eternal Father deceiveth us not. Sons labour, that they may receive the inheritance of their parents, to whom when dead they are to succeed: are we not labouring to receive an inheritance from that Father, to whom not dying we succeed; but together with Him in the very inheritance for everlasting are to live?"
> – Augustine, Expositions on the Psalms, 61

Diving In

Read, at a minimum, Matthew 1:1 - 2:23 and Luke 1:27 - 3:38

Joseph.

He is mentioned briefly in only three Gospels yet we know more about his ancestors and the ancestors of his wife than most any other person in the Bible. We know his hometown, his marital plans, his travel plans, details of the birth of his first son and we know his occupation. We know he had other sons and daughters and we know he died before his wife and children. We know God spoke to him at least three times through an angel and directed his physical and emotional paths in life.

But we don't know what he said. Not a single word.

The earthly father of the Lord Jesus is never quoted in the Bible, either directly or indirectly. Instead, his value as protector over the life of the baby Jesus is one of his critical roles in the story. In contrast to the earthly father, Jesus once said this, "I speak just as the Father taught me."

Perhaps there is a truly significant lesson in the life of Joseph for all fathers – that they seek to not be remembered for what they said, but for what they taught their children that their Father in heaven has said.

Question
1. What were Jacob's fears?
2. Did Jacob live a fearless life in the Lord?
3. How does this story impact the story of your life?

44

Matthew 10:26 "Fear not them."

Read first: Matthew 10:26-33

The 'them' to which Jesus refers are the 'wolves' or the men who will flog the disciples, drag the disciples before secular rulers, hate the disciples, and bear false witness against the disciples by saying they, along with Jesus, are in league with the devil. This is a long litany of assured abuses which face the disciples, yet they are told by their Master to "Fear not!"

Jesus is likely teaching the difference between fear and discomfort, between being afraid of injustice and enduring it. Is it easier to face the beatings and repudiations if you know they are coming? Perhaps not, but it does tend to take the element of surprise out of them. If we know someone is coming to rail on us, we can prepare ourselves and focus upon surviving the attack.

Jesus adds a reason of hope to this "Fear not!" when he says that, "nothing is hidden that will not be uncovered and nothing is secret that will not be known". In other words, there is an accounting to be had in the future. Records are being kept now and God's judgment will be forthcoming. We need not fear that men who hate God will 'get away with it'. We need not fear their power or appearance of power. We need not fear because they have an end, while we who endure will be saved to eternal life. Proverbs 11:21 says, "Be assured, an evil person will not go unpunished, but the offspring of the righteous will be delivered."

Prayer: Talk with your Father in heaven about placing judgment and punishment in His hands and forgiveness and grace in your hands.

> "For when grace has come, and driven away the darkness of the understanding, we learn the exact nature of things, and what was before dreadful to us becomes contemptible. For we no longer fear death, after learning exactly, from this sacred initiation, that death is not death, but a sleep and a seasonable slumber; nor poverty nor disease, nor any other such thing, knowing that we are on our way to a better life, undefiled and incorruptible, and free from all such vicissitudes."
> – John Chrysostom, Instructions to Catechumens

Diving In

Read, at a minimum, Matthew 2, 14, Luke 23, Acts 12

Herod.

The name is synonymous with evil. Herod the Great massacred the infants in Bethlehem, Herod Antipas beheaded John the Baptist, Herod Agrippa I put James to death and Peter on death row.

Yet for all their wickedness, we are told their underlying fears were not so uncommon. Herod the Great was afraid of losing authority, power, and influence. Most everyone, from parents to politicians experience this concern. Herod Antipas was afraid of embarrassment and demonstrating weakness and ineptitude. Most everyone has made a rash statement or promise without having given full thought to the consequences. (No intimate information about Herod Agrippa I is revealed in Scripture but given the description of his other actions he appears to have been fully given to evil.)

Historically the entire Herodian family was a dysfunctional mess of murder, betrayal, lies, deceit, wrongful marriage, lust, and maniacal misuse of power. This type of behavior in families has been repeated in every age and culture, unfortunately. Perhaps the history of the family of Herod is included in Scripture as a warning – both about avoiding these attitudes and behaviors and about how these types of families are likely to persecute the Christian church.

Question

1. What were Herod's fears? (Do we not all have fears of embarrassment?)
2. Did Herod live a fearless life in the Lord?
3. How does this story impact the story of your life?

45

Matthew 10:28, Luke 12:4 "Fear not those who kill the body."

Read first: Matthew 10:26-33

This word of Jesus is intended for those in the middle of torturous attacks and for those who are facing a severe challenge to their faith under physical persecution. Impending death is nothing compared to the reality of eternal death and therefore we must flee for mercy to him who controls this eternal destiny rather than to him who has been given permission to end this earthly life.

More than this we are taught that there is a body and there is a soul and that the two, while intertwined on this level of existence, are separable. One is mortal, temporal. The other is immortal, spiritual. Where does our person-hood, our reason, our faith, exist? Jesus is teaching that it truly exists in, or as, the soul. However, we are often misinformed, or confused, and believe that these exist as an inseparable part of our flesh and blood.

If we do not fear those who kill the body, our fear must be

placed somewhere else – for to fear is human. If our fear is in God we live as spiritual persons, bound not by the sin and corruption which is our genetic inheritance, but bound by the inheritance of a promise made by our Creator and our Redeemer. If we fear him who has all authority over body and soul, what is sickness, what is malady, what is deformity? Are we not more than these? Are we not souls to be looked at with inestimable value and nurtured with the everlasting words of hope, peace, forgiveness, and restoration? Yes, yes we are!

Prayer: Praise your Father in heaven for His creation which is you, both your body and soul.

> "The last times are come upon us. Let us therefore be of a reverent spirit, and fear the long-suffering of God, lest we despise the riches of His goodness and forbearance. For let us either fear the wrath to come, or let us love the present joy in the life that now is; and let our present and true joy be only this, to be found in Christ Jesus, that we may truly live. Do not at any time desire so much as even to breathe apart from Him. For He is my hope; He is my boast; He is my never-failing riches."
> – Ignatius, The Epistle to the Ephesians

Diving In

Read, at a minimum, Matthew 3, 11, 14, Luke 1, 3, 7, John 1

John the Baptist.

His birth was nothing short of a miracle. His death nothing short of gross injustice. He wore clothing of camel's hair and a leather belt. He ate meals of grasshoppers sweetened with wild honey. He preached of Judgment Day and condemned unholy actions of both political and religious leaders. He stood in the waters of the Jordan and people joined him in repentance. But his greatest act was baptizing the Son of God.

John knew his mission was to preach repentance; his purpose to go before the One to come. Yet John was not altogether clear on the details. He was reluctant to baptize Jesus, he did not believe he himself was Elijah, he became doubtful that Jesus was the One to come.

Jesus saw John as much more than John saw himself. Jesus wanted John to help him fulfill righteousness. Jesus taught that John was the promised Elijah to come. Jesus comforted John's doubts with hard evidence. And about John, Jesus said, "Among those born of women, none is greater than John."

A quiet burial marked the end of his life. His disciples and his Lord mourned his execution; he had no immediate family.

Question
1. What were John's fears?
2. Did John live a fearless life in the Lord?
3. How does this story impact the story of your life?

46

Matthew 10:31, Luke 12:7 "Fear not! You are of more value than many sparrows."

Read first: Matthew 10:26-33

This is a "Fear not!" by comparison of value. Jesus has previously taught: "Look at the birds of the air: they neither sow nor reap nor gather into barns, and yet your heavenly Father feeds them." Now he teaches, "Are not two sparrows sold for a penny? And not one of them will fall to the ground apart from your Father." Therefore, if God cares for (not just about) birds, does he not care for you? Since the answer is yes, then you should not fear surviving this life or dying unnoticed.

So we are to fear neither living nor dying. That about covers it all, doesn't it? But the comparison Jesus makes is the great value of this "Fear not!" Where can you go that you will not find a bird? They are everywhere on the planet, from the desert to the Antarctic, from the rain forest to the city. Everywhere there is a visible, tangible, audible reminder of our value! If the birds are fed by God, is it reasonable for us to fear our nutritional needs? If no bird dies apart from the will of God, is it rational for us to ever think we have been abandoned?

The next time we are afraid of something, perhaps it would be good to get out and find a bird; they have much to teach us about how our Father wants us to feel and live.

Prayer: Praise your heavenly Father for the birds – and ask Him to teach you about the ones that are nearby you every day.

> "For what comfort have I left but that I hope to come quickly to thee, my brother, and that thy departure will not cause a long severance between us. For who is there who ought not to wish for himself beyond all else that 'this corruptible should put on in-corruption, and this mortal put on immortality'? that we who succumb to death through the frailty of the body, being raised above nature, may no longer have to fear death."
> – Ambrose, On the Decease of Saytrus, Book II

Diving In

Read, at a minimum, Matthew 10:26-33

Peter.

Peter leaps off the pages of the Gospels as the most colorful and dynamic character besides Jesus. He is bold and boisterous. He is as passionate about his convictions as he is predictable in his thinking. And more than this, his confession becomes the Rock upon which the church is founded.

Peter is an ordinary sort of man; he has a job, a family, friends. Then along comes Jesus and everything changes: his job, his family and his friends. And Jesus scares him, perplexes him and awes him. Jesus scared him in the boat after catching so many fish, Jesus perplexes him by almost walking by the boat on the water and Jesus awes him by awakening in the boat and calming the storm. Yet Peter is the only disciple recorded to have said, "No!" to Jesus. He is recorded as violently defending Jesus. And he is recorded as weeping over his betrayal of Jesus.

It is after all of these things that Peter is restored and sent by Jesus to "feed my sheep" and care for the new believers in Christ the Lord. After a twisting roller coaster ride through the Gospels we are left with the story of man who in many respects is all of us put together; called, broken and restored in the Lord Jesus.

Question
1. What were Peter's fears in the Gospels?
2. Did Peter live a fearless life in the Lord?
3. How does this story impact the story of your life?

47

Matthew 14:27, Mark 6:50, John 6:20 "It is I. Fear not!"

Read first: Matthew 14:22-33

There is a level of astonishment to this "Fear not!" and a level of compassion worthy of reflection. As for the astonishment, let us remember it was night and very windy. Mark records the time as the fourth watch, some of the blackest time of night, and the disciples had been on the sea since evening. John tells us they were about three or four miles from shore, placing them near the middle of the sea. The sea was rough and the disciples were kind of stuck; Mark tells us that Jesus noticed the disciples were making a very slow traverse of the sea. Then, from the disciple's point of view, along comes a man. Not in a boat. Walking. In the middle of the sea. Walking on water, really rough water.

Two reactions would be normal in this situation: incredulity or fear. Given that seamen have historically been a somewhat superstitious bunch, and given that they were pulling an all-nighter and were physically exhausted, this sight of a man walking on water never entered the realm of wonder but took up residence in the land of terror. Jesus immediately speaks with compassion and tells them to "Fear not!" Amazingly the voice of the apparition produces a level of calm in the disciples, enough that Peter calls out to his Lord for permission to join him on the water. After Peter is saved by Jesus and Jesus gets into the boat the wind stops – a jaw-dropping change in the weather.

Every once in a while, and sometimes not even in a lifetime, a person is astounded by someone they thought they knew. It could be a friend who evidences a level of knowledge or physical strength which was never imagined to exist. The friend knew of their ability all along but never felt it necessary to demonstrate it. And the level to which the friend has risen makes the other person feel very small, almost unworthy to be in his friendship; for what reason would this awesome friend have of such small companionship or weak insights and assistance. This is the experience the disciples had.

Jesus certainly had already done amazing things but walking on water demonstrates a power far beyond making food miraculously appear or making diseases miraculously disappear. This is openly divine power and what happens when divine power is revealed to mortal man? It causes fear in us. And as the angels who visited Gideon and Daniel, Jesus speaks compassionately to the disciples. "Fear not! It is I!" This 'I' is here to save, take heart, there is no fear in Him.

Prayer: Ask your Father in heaven to open your eyes to where He is displaying His mighty power and to where He is displaying His mighty compassion.

Diving In

Read, at a minimum, Matthew 14:22-33

Peter.

Peter does not leap off the pages of the Acts of the Apostles as he did in the Gospels. While he does hold sway in the early chapters, most of the book is given to the dynamic life and times of Paul the apostle. It is in the early chapters, however, that we meet a calmer and more clear-headed Peter.

The Peter we meet in Acts is almost a different man altogether from the one in the Gospels. Peter first leads in prayer – which he never does in the Gospels. Then in speech – which he did in the Gospels but nearly always in foolhardy way. Then in witness – which he did in the Gospels but then made the mistake of rebuking Jesus. And later he leads in the discovery of the global reach of the good news of Jesus the Christ.

The Peter of Acts is a man unafraid; unafraid of Jesus, of the enemies of Jesus, even of the friends of Jesus. The Peter of Acts is knowledgeable, dependable, and patient. What a change Jesus made in Peter in just a few short years!

Question
1. What were Peter's fears in the Acts of the Apostles?
2. Did Peter live a fearless life in the Lord?
3. How does this story impact the story of your life?

48

Matthew 17:7 "Jesus touched them and said, 'Rise and fear not!'"

Read first: Matthew 17:1-13

Seeing the unveiled majesty of God tends to produce a dirty face. Abraham, Ezekiel, Daniel (twice), Peter, James, John (twice) all fall on their face when they see or hear God. Moses and Elijah both hid their faces – when they were living on earth, not when they visited with Jesus on the mountain. This isn't just a shield your eyes or turn your face, no, this is a total body reaction akin to the proverbial ostrich burying his head in the sand.

Interestingly, in almost every case, the dirty-faced man is asked to rise. God, while apparently unperturbed by the physical reaction to his presence, prefers to speak to his creation when it is standing upright. This says a great deal about our relationship to God our Creator. God values humbleness but not distance. He despises sin but encourages dialogue. God wants a heartfelt and intimate relationship with his children, one based upon grace and peace, reverence, passionate commitment and expectation of growth. We were made to stand on our two feet, not in pride but in service to the King of kings.

It is touching (pun intended) that Jesus would touch his disciples and tell them to rise and "Fear not!" God is fairly touchy-feely; he likes a hands-on approach. God formed Adam and breathed into his nostrils. Daniel was touched and asked to rise, Isaiah's and Jeremiah's lips were touched, John was touched during his vision (recorded in Revelation). Jesus touched the children, the lepers, the dead, and the living. There is something about touch which brings reassurance (think of Thomas touching the hands and side of Jesus). Bottom line, God knows our fears and knows exactly how to comfort us. Thank God for his love and grace!

Prayer: Talk with your Father in heaven about times when He has touched you, either through an angelic messenger or a human representative.

> "What one wishes to receive, in order to turn to an improper use, God in His mercy rather refuses to bestow. Moreover, if a man asks what would, if answered, only tend to his injury, there is surely greater cause to fear, lest what God could not withhold with kindness, He should give in His anger."
> – Augustine, Tractates on John, LXXIII

Diving In

Read, at a minimum, 1 and 2 Peter

Peter.

The New Testament contains two letters by Peter. These letters are a product of his life and service to Jesus. While Peter does not regale us with a play-by-play of historical events, he does include many references to significant experiences he had with Jesus.

In light of these experiences, Peter is able to share his living hope of the resurrection, his understanding of trials and persecutions, his role and the role of the ancient prophets in God's plan of salvation, and the necessity of recognizing evil and being prepared to both counter it and suffer under it.

Peter's letters come from a heart renewed by faith and a life given to Jesus. In the sum of all Peter had become, his one goal was to communicate Jesus the Lord. In doing so, he encouraged and exhorted believers and feed the sheep God had given to him. A great tree had grown up from the Rock of Peter's confession and it was now bearing fruit for the blessing of God's people.

Question

1. What were Peter's fears about the future of Christ's church?
2. How did Peter encourage others to live a fearless life in the Lord?
3. How do his letters set an example for you about the story of your life?

49

Matthew 28:5 "Fear not!"

Read first: Matthew 28:1-10

What's there to be afraid of? Earthquakes? Angels who look like lightning? Soldiers who fall to the ground like dead men? A dead man come back to life? I love the simplicity of angels. Their plain understanding of events is surpassed only by their apparent innocence about our human condition.

"Fear not!" the angel says to women who no doubt are trembling uncontrollably. Emotionally wasted, their senses are now overwhelmed by things never before seen by any man or woman. "Fear not!" he says, "For I know that you seek Jesus – who was brutally tortured and murdered." Not the best of openers for a human to hear. "Don't be afraid while I remind you of the terror and pain of the last couple of days." (It's like a young brother regaling to his sister his worst experience at the doctor in an effort to provide reassurance that her visit will be okay.) "He's not here! Just like he said! Come and see." (You know, if the women have come to see Jesus, it may not be too helpful to point out that he is GONE! But this is the innocence of angels.)

This "Fear not!" is about how what the women (and we) see is open to a much different interpretation. What would seem to be fearful – angels, dead soldiers, missing Jesus – is actually not. The angel, while visually startling, is a messenger of great news! The soldiers, while scary and intimidating in their own right, have been nullified by the angel. The missing Jesus, while mystifying and unsettling, actually testifies to the truth of all he said and illuminates the glorious future for all who believe what he said. Fear is the lens through which the women were viewing the world (and understandably so). The angel of God asks them to look instead with the eyes of fearless trust. And when they did, they "ran with fear and great joy to the disciples".

How much of what we fear can be overcome with the perspective of an angel?

Prayer: Ask your Father in heaven for the 'perspective of an angel'.

Diving In

Read, at a minimum, Matthew 28:1-10

Soldiers.

Underneath the armor and the brutality, every soldier is still a human being. Both the violent life and questioning soul of soldiers are presented to us in the Bible. Soldiers arrested, mocked, beat and crucified Jesus. They broke the legs of criminals and speared Jesus. But military men also came to John the Baptist for instruction on how to be a good and decent soldiers. The centurion came to Jesus humble under His authority. Soldiers defended Paul and listened to his counsel to save their lives and the lives of their prisoners.

Soldiers are also used as illustrations and descriptors of the Christian life. Believers have spiritual armor to put on, we are called to suffer as a 'soldier of Christ Jesus' and Epaphroditus and Archippus are 'fellow soldiers' of Paul.

In every age there are military personnel who face fears and doubts many of us will never know. Yet service, honor, submission to authority, hard work, and dauntless courage are attributes every Christian should know, and wear, well.

Question
1. What were soldier's fears?
2. Could a / Can a soldier live a fearless life in the Lord?
3. How does this career impact the story of your life?

50

Matthew 28:10 "Fear not!"

Read first: Matthew 28:1-10

Many people have properly understood this "Fear Not!", along with Jesus words to Mary (recorded in John 20), as the women being afraid that Jesus would leave them again. They apparently gripped pretty hard on to him and he had to politely extract himself. Accepting the fact of the resurrection, which they had witnessed with Lazarus and heard about (no doubt) with the young man from Nain, they knew Jesus to be really alive and they did not ever want to part from him again. The treasure that he was to them surpassed all their understanding and filled their hearts so that all they wanted to do was hold on forever. We can so appreciate how they felt. If we had someone we loved in like measure brought back from the dead, we too would cling on to them with all our strength.

However, Jesus dragging several women along behind him

was not a very practical way to accomplish the rest of the visits he had to do. So Jesus tells them to "Fear not!" because death no longer has a hold over Jesus (or them). He has now fulfilled the will of his Father and he will be with his disciples (through the power and presence of the Holy Spirit) forever. No need to cling, Jesus won't ever be away again.

To release Jesus took an enormous amount of trust. Not that coming back from the dead doesn't engender such trust. It's just that these were such powerful emotions and such mind-boggling events. So many centuries later, the events and emotions do not seem as colossal. Maybe that is okay – but only because the directive "Go and tell." has not lost any of its great importance. Great messages do not always have to be delivered with great emotion; the message itself can produce all the necessary inspiration.

Prayer: Ask your heavenly Father to inspire you to greater trust.

> "It is enough for women to protect their locks, and bind up their hair simply along the neck with a plain hair-pin, nourishing chaste locks with simple care to true beauty. For meretricious plaiting of the hair, and putting it up in tresses, contribute to make them look ugly, cutting the hair and plucking off it those treacherous braidings; on account of which they do not touch their head, being afraid of disordering their hair. Sleep, too, comes on, not without fear lest they pull down without knowing the shape of the braid."
> – Clement of Alexandria, The Instructor, Book III

Diving In

Read, at a minimum, Matthew 28:1-10

Women.

Jesus and the women who followed and ministered to him had a special relationship. The Gospels do not give us many details but they remind us that women, and a particular group of women, were with Jesus continually.

Three to four women appear to have been regular followers of Jesus and the same were with Jesus as he died on the cross. These women provided for the disciples and Jesus out of their own pockets, giving of their time and energy as well. There were also 'many others' who probably came and went as their family's needs allowed and these were likely those among the disciples on the day of Pentecost. The women were additionally devoted to prayer, not just service and giving.

Jesus healed, taught and blessed many women. He healed a woman of demons, a woman with twelve years of illness, and a woman bent over double. He taught the 'woman at the well' and the Canaanite woman. Jesus blessed Mary and Martha with the resurrection of Lazarus, the mother at Nain with the resurrection of her son, and a mother and father with the resurrection of their twelve-year-old daughter.

The first people to see Jesus and hear Jesus speak after his resurrection were women. They also were the first to touch the Risen Lord and the first to be tasked with the good news: "Go and tell my brothers. . ."

Question
1. What were the women's fears?
2. Did the women live a fearless life in the Lord?
3. How does their experience impact the story of your life?

51

Mark 5:36, Luke 8:50 "Fear not, only believe."

Read first: Mark 5:21-43

I recently read a father's story about almost losing his son. He had this to say about the experience (and I paraphrase), "While I scolded God about taking my son from me, he was sitting in the lap of Jesus the whole time." This father's insight was that while he, in his moment of unrighteous anger, accused God of not caring for his son, the fact was that his son could not have been held in more caring arms.

The loss of a child is perhaps the most devastating tragedy a parent can endure. The synagogue ruler was facing this tragedy when Jesus said "Fear not!" After coming to the itinerant rabbi and literally begging at his feet for him to come heal his daughter the father was made to endure delay. Many a father can attest to the irritation, impatience, and insult he feels when health care is delayed for his child. You feel ready to tear down doors and walls to get your child to the doctor for immediate care. The father of the twelve year old girl was delayed by a woman who had somehow been healed by Jesus and to whom Jesus seemed compelled to listen as she told her whole life's story. While this was going on a servant of the father came and told him that his daughter was dead.

The fear of truth surely rose in the father's heart like the mushroom cloud of a nuclear detonation. We can imagine him looking from the servant to Jesus (wondering why he delayed) to the woman (wondering if this was her fault) to the crowd (wondering if they felt his pain) and back to the servant again (wondering if this was all a nightmare he would soon awaken from). Into this father's fear came the voice of God, "Fear not, only believe!"

Believe what? Believe what you cannot see. Believe in God. We need not live in fear when our children are held in the arms of Jesus. They are not lost, though they die. We are wounded but are not left without a Healer and Comforter. We believe what we cannot see but which is nevertheless reality. We are held in the arms, once wounded but now healed, of Jesus.

Prayer: Talk with your Father in heaven about these words from the disciple Peter, "Though you have not seen him, you love him. Though you do not now see him, you believe in him and rejoice with joy that is inexpressible and filled with glory, obtaining the outcome of your faith, the salvation of your souls."

Diving In

Read, at a minimum, Mark 5:21-43

James.

James was the older brother. A son of Zebedee, Jesus called James and his brother the Sons of Thunder. Along with his brother and Peter, James was witness to some of the most fantastic events: the resurrection of the twelve-year-old girl, the transfiguration of Jesus on the mountain, their Lord in desperate prayer.

James was not one to hedge his questions. At one time he asked Jesus to let him sit next to Jesus in glory. Another time he asked for signs of the coming destruction of Jerusalem. Yet another time he asked if he was supposed to call down fire from heaven upon people who had rejected Jesus.

A fisherman by trade, he did not die on a boat or in a storm but by the hand of Herod who simply felt like killing followers of Jesus.

Question
1. What were the fears of James?
2. Did James live a fearless life in the Lord?
3. How does his story impact the story of your life?

52

Luke 1:13 "Fear not for your prayer has been heard."

Read first: Luke 1:5-23

Most of us get startled when we know we are alone and we turn around (or look up) and there is someone standing there looking at us. This surprise can happen with someone we know or a complete stranger. But to look up and see and angel staring at you would certainly make the heart skip a couple of beats.

Zechariah is really alone. The space he was in was totally enclosed – one way in, one way out, and very, very off limits. Zechariah looks up and there is an angel. Maybe not the nicest thing to do to an old man – could have given him a heart attack. But then, there is the angelic way of thinking: I was looking at you, human, the whole time, what's the big deal that you can see me now? Didn't you know I was here all along?

So Zechariah is greatly distressed and the angel is, well, nearly giddy. It's the angelic way again. Gabriel is totally excited to bring the good news to Zechariah that God's answer to his prayer is yes, and yes in a big way. This visit from heaven is not a heralding of disaster but a proclamation of fulfillment. What's to fear? – the forerunner of the Messiah is near! And you will have joy and gladness and many will rejoice and oh, here are some parenting tips, and he will be great and filled with the Holy Spirit and he'll do great things and move men's hearts and oh, there is the Elijah connection and . . . .

Zechariah's head must have been spinning. You go from terror to terrific in less than 30 seconds, carried along by Divine joy. Now honestly, not all our prayers will receive such answers, but all of our prayers are heard. Never fear, God is near, and hears all we say to him. And who knows? Maybe that angel will reveal himself!

Prayer: Talk with your Father in heaven about talking with Him, that your conversation may be deeper and richer every day, filled with repentance and joy.

"Unreasoning creatures are far better than we both in habit of body, and in independence; they fear no poverty."
– John Chrysostom, Homilies on Philippians VII

Diving In

Read, at a minimum, Luke 1:5-23

Zechariah.

Zechariah's brief appearance in the Biblical record is a journey from speech to silence to inspired speech.

Beginning with his prayers and worship in the temple, we learn that Zechariah is a man of speech. He is a priest and therefore his life is one of teaching and leading the people. However, after a relatively brief conversation with the angel Gabriel, Zechariah is made mute. For the next nine months he is unable to utter a word while the herald of the Messiah develops in his wife's womb.

Suddenly at his son's circumcision, Zechariah speaks his first words in almost a year and he blesses God. Filled with the Holy Spirit, Zechariah proclaims a beautiful psalm to God and a blessing to his son John.

Question
1. What were Zechariah's fears?
2. Did Zechariah's words, or lack thereof, demonstrate a fearless life in the Lord?
3. How does his story of speech and silence impact the story of your life?

53

Luke 1:30 "Fear not for you have found favor with God."

Read first: Luke 1:26-33

We can only speculate why Gabriel chose to address Mary differently than Zechariah. His first words to Zechariah were "Fear not!" To Mary he said, "Greetings O favored one, the Lord is with you!" However, the result was the same – both were pretty upset.

In Zechariah's case, the Greek word is 'tarasso' which means 'to be greatly distressed'. In Mary's case, the Greek word is a synonym for 'tarasso' and it is 'diatarassomai' which carries a meaning of something like 'to have acute or deep distress'. This is Gabriel's fourth time out – at least as recorded in the Bible. First two times he made Daniel fall on his face, now he's scared an old man and a young woman. Not a very auspicious track record! In a way we might feel sorry for Gabriel – no matter what he says or does he scares people.

Are all angels this scary? Is there one in the Bible that wasn't? Consider the angel in the Garden of Eden, the angel who spoke with Gideon and Manoah, the angels who destroyed Sodom and Gomorrah, the 'terror of the night' in Psalm 91, or the angel(s) who came to Isaiah, Daniel, the women at the tomb, Zechariah, Mary. Only Peter (when he was in prison) and Paul (on the island of Cauda) seem to have had fearless angelic visits. Yet, in every case, the people of God were protected, blessed, delivered, given good news, or encouraged by these visits.

Simple fact is that the core of our being knows that we cannot stand in the presence of God. The unspoken truth in every cell of our body is that we are in rebellion against our Creator and deserve nothing but total destruction. Into this reality comes the grace, mercy and forgiveness of God. Into this life of death comes the word "Fear not!" because since we can do nothing to save ourselves, God has saved us and sent messengers to tell us what he has done. Some of these messengers are men, some are angels but the message of hope, love and promise is the same: "Fear not!"

Prayer: Talk with your Father in heaven about prisoners for the Lord and ask Him to send His angels to comfort and encourage them.

> "Where the fear of God is, there is seriousness, an honourable and yet thoughtful diligence, as well as an anxious carefulness and a well-considered admission to the sacred ministry and a safely-guarded communion, and promotion after good service, and a scrupulous submission to authority, and a devout attendance, and a modest gait, and a united church, and God in all things."
> – Tertullian, The Prescription Against Heritics

Diving In

Read, at a minimum, Luke 1:26-33

Mary.

Mary's life was one of loss and hope. At first, Mary loses the favor of her husband Joseph when she is found to be with child. Soon after hearing from an angel, Joseph returns and the hope of a good marriage returns with him. Not much later, Mary loses the comforts of her home village by being forced to travel to Bethlehem and then loses the comforts of her country as she is forced to travel to, and live in, Egypt. They do return later, however, to their own country and their own hometown. A number of years later, they lose Jesus on a trip from Jerusalem. Hoping against hope they return to the big city to search for him and they do indeed find him, safe and sound.

At some point, and we are not told when, she loses her husband Joseph. She is not destitute, however, for she has both sons and daughters. Yet, at another point, she loses her firstborn son. The Bible records, "And when his family heard it, they went out to seize Jesus, for they were saying, 'He is out of his mind.'" The Bible also records that when Mary went to see Jesus with her children, he indicated that his mother and brother were not biological but anyone who did the will of God. Still, Mary was not without hope because her son healed the sick, blind and paralyzed, taught with authority, resurrected the dead and fed thousands of men, women and children.

Mary's most devastating loss was certainly the death of her son, viciously and unmercifully tortured and crucified. Yet even at this dark hour, Jesus did not leave her without hope but placed her in the care of the disciple he loved.

Finally, in a strange reversal of loss and hope, Mary finds her son alive, resurrected from the dead. But then she loses him again, this time as he goes to his Father in heaven.

Question

1. What were Mary's fears?
2. Did Mary live a fearless life in the Lord?
3. How does Mary's story impact the story of your life?

54

Luke 2:10 "Fear not for I bring you good news."

Read first: Luke 2:8-14

  The shepherds, while potentially devout Jews, were probably not expecting an angelic visit that night – any more than any other night of their humble lives. The glory of the Lord which was shining around them was certainly as mysterious as it was bright. That the shepherds remembered the words of the angels later seems remarkable, even divinely provisioned, given their great fear.

  One unique aspect to this "Fear not!" is that previously Zechariah and Mary were distressed by the angel's appearance but in this case the shepherds were fearing with a great fear (mega phobos). This description of the shepherd's fear matches more closely with those who felt they were going to die at seeing God rather than Zechariah and Mary who, while disturbed, did not appear to fear for their lives.

  The shepherds likely did not immediately cease fearing when the angel said "Fear not!". Instead, their feelings of fear likely began to dissipate when, or after, they had been sung to. Honestly, how many scary bad people sing praises to God after they have scared someone? Eventually their fear would give way to praising God for all that 'they had heard and seen as it had been told to them'. So, while the delivery method may have been emotionally overpowering, the message was kept intact – which is the most important part in the end.

Prayer: Sing to your Father in heaven.

> "The adversary had leapt forth to disturb the camp of Christ with violent terror; but he was beaten back and conquered; and as much fear and terror as he had brought, so much bravery and strength he also found. He had thought that he could again overthrow the servants of God, and agitate them in his accustomed manner, as if they were novices and inexperienced-as if little prepared and little cautious. He attacked one first, as a wolf had tried to separate the sheep from the flock; for he who has not sufficient strength against all, seeks to gain advantage from the solitude of individuals. But when beaten back as well by the faith as by the vigour of the combined army, he perceived that the soldiers of Christ are now watching, and stand sober and armed for the battle; that they cannot be conquered, but that they can die; and that by this very fact they are invincible, that they do not fear death; that they do not in turn assail their assailants, since it is not lawful for the innocent even to kill the guilty; but that they readily deliver up both their lives and their blood; that since such malice and cruelty rages in the world, they may the more quickly withdraw from the evil and cruel. What a glorious spectacle was that under the eyes of God!"
> – Cyprian, Epistle LVI. ca. 250A.D.

Diving In

Read, at a minimum, Luke 2:8-14

Shepherds.

Shepherding. It was an occupation. It did have noble roots, however. The patriarchs, Abraham, Isaac and Jacob were all shepherds. Even Moses tended flocks for 40 years. The Psalms called the Lord "my shepherd" and the "Shepherd of Israel". The great king David was a shepherd in his younger years.

Of course, the Egyptians considered shepherds an abomination. And most people didn't want to be around shepherds – sheep, and those who care for them, did not have a pleasant smell. It didn't take a great deal of intelligence or imagination to be a shepherd. It did take a bit of bravado, but usually just false bravado – enough 'show' to scare off the occasional wolf or lion hunting for a meal.

But shepherds were necessary. There were a lot of uses for a sheep, especially when a sacrifice was needed. And Passover, well, that required a great many lambs.

Suddenly, one night, a select group of shepherds saw things in the sky, heard things told to them, discovered a baby lying in a manger. They were excited for a while, telling everyone what they had seen and heard. But after a while the excitement died down. The sheep needed new pasture. And life went on.

Question
1. What were shepherd's fears?
2. Can a shepherd live a fearless life in the Lord?
3. How does this career impact the story of your life?

55

Luke 5:10 "Fear not; from now on you will be catching men."

Read first: Luke 5:1-11

Many a preacher has disparaged Simon Peter for his reaction to Jesus in the boat. However, such men should also ridiculously ridicule Isaiah for his outburst when he saw the Lord seated on his throne. Peter fell in line with all other humble sinners who realize they are in the presence of their holy Creator; he knows he is sinful and unworthy and deserving only of eternal death. As Jesus did not criticize Peter for his fear neither should we. Instead Simon is encouraged by the words of his Lord to "Fear not!" because Simon is told he will be used as an instrument by God to bring in a portion of the harvest. God has had mercy upon this sinner and wishes that he be used for the glory of the kingdom of God.

This mercy is what makes this "Fear not!", and so many others, so beautiful. Gideon was used as an instrument of deliverance for God's people. Mary was used as an instrument to bring the flesh and blood of the Savior to this world. Simon is used as the firstborn of all pastors and missionaries who bring the good news to sinful men and women.

This "Fear not!" applies not only to the holy / sinful dynamic between Jesus and Simon but also to their relationship. Simon is to have a fear-less attitude toward his Lord; he is to feel free to approach his Master with his needs, questions, concerns, hopes and dreams. Simon is to not be afraid in following his Lord where He leads. Of all the people who heard "Fear not!" it is Simon who was meant to hear it as the defining characteristic of the rest of his life. And perhaps this is how Simon heard it, for while he did stumble from time to time, he always rebounded to a life lived more fully to his Savior Jesus.

Prayer: Talk with your Father in heaven about times when He held you up when you stumbled, carried you when you could not walk.

"Call thy son, and frighten him, and threaten to lay a few stripes upon him, if he does not duly observe your law; and thou wilt see, how he will forthwith abstain. Is it not therefore truly absurd, that little children, out of the fear we inspire, should obey us, and that we should not fear God as our sons fear us?"

– John Chrysostom, Homilies Concerning the Statues XIX

Diving In

Read, at a minimum, Luke 5:1-11

Judas.

It took only minutes and the name was forever connected to betrayal.

He was "one of the twelve" and not some stranger or outsider. The son of Simon Iscariot, he was in charge of the group's finances and was already known to be a thief. What no one knew was the depths to which he would go to get money. Selling the Rabbi to the religious leaders who hated him was so unconscionable, so unholy, that no one suspected him – even when the Rabbi told him to go and do quickly what he was going to do.

But sell is what Judas did. He sold Jesus for a very large sum of money, enough money to buy a farm. But this self-indulgent criminal did not count on one thing getting in his way: his conscience.

A sudden and fierce pang of guilt struck Judas and when he tried to repair the damage he had done, he found out that those to whom he sold the Rabbi had less conscience than he did. Finally laid bare for all the world to see, Judas' sin drove him to complete despair. He committed suicide by hanging himself.

Question
1. What were the fears of Judas?
2. Did Judas live a fearless life in the Lord?
3. How do the choices Judas made impact the story of your life?

56

Luke 12:32 "Fear not, little flock."

Read first: Luke 12:23-34

This "Fear not!" is specific to the kingdom of heaven. The little flock should not fear being unable to find God's kingdom because it is the Father's good pleasure to give it to them. Also, by extension, they need not fear for clothing or food because these will be given to those who seek/possess God's kingdom. Jesus sets up here a win-win scenario. What you look for you will find and when you find it you will have what you need.

Living in God's kingdom is a different matter than finding it, however. Jesus has us consider in this teaching the characteristic of anxious living. What are the concerns of this life and why do we trouble ourselves over them? "They are so small!" says our Lord. "Put your energies into God the Father's way of thinking, doing, speaking and the little things will be given to you by Him."

Parents know this dynamic firsthand. A child will often weep, or express anguish, or brood over the simplest of things; a misplaced scrap of paper, a piece of candy thrown away, a favorite shirt which must be washed. In the same way our Father in heaven sees as minor concerns many of the things we see as major issues. Moreover, a defining difference between what we see and what God sees is fear. Many times we fear what we feel we cannot control. God would like us to feel comfort in placing our desire for control into his hands. In much the same way that paper can be replaced, candy procured and clothing returned, God feels more than adequate to the task of caring for all our needs.

Let us not fear, then, to trust Him for all we need. Instead, let us seek His authority and He will show us His mighty blessings.

Prayer: Ask your Father in heaven to take control from you as you seek His kingdom.

> "The Law was given that, through fear of punishment, it might recall those who were wandering beyond the limits of nature, to their observance, but grace to incite the elect both by the desire of good things, and also by the promised rewards."
> – Ambrose, Concerning Widows

Diving In

Read, at a minimum, Luke 12:23-34

Pharisees.

As a group, and grouped together with the scribes, Sadducees, and teachers of the law, the Pharisees were the bitter enemies of Jesus. The Pharisees called him the devil; Jesus called them 'a brood of vipers' and hypocrites. The Pharisees tried to test, trap and destroy Jesus. Jesus compared them to whitewashed tombs and said they were full of greed and wickedness.

The Pharisees knew Jesus performed miracles of healing and knew that Jesus understood the Scriptures better than they did so they plotted with their opposition, the Sadducees, and tried to discredit him and arrest him. Every attempt failed. Except for the one that involved Judas.

Yet there were two Pharisees who did not fit the mold: Nicodemus and Paul. One would help bury Jesus, the other would die for Jesus.

Question
1. What were the fears of the Pharisees?
2. Could a Pharisee live a fearless life in the Lord?
3. How does this career impact the story of your life?

57

Acts 18:9 "Fear not them but go on speaking."

Read first: Acts 18:1-11

There were many times Paul had a healthy fear of being beaten, stoned, or thrown to his death. This fear motivated him to move on to the next town and share God's good news there. In the case of Corinth, God knew something Paul did not and so he came to Paul to tell him to stay – which Paul did for a year and a half.

This "Fear not!" presents an insight to the many times when people were in fear of their lives and God came to tell them to "Fear not!" Fear can sometimes be a feeling (perception) used by God for good; as in Paul's case where it kept him and the Gospel message on the move. In other cases, God would have us not fear but stand fast. In these cases God desires to work his will in the present circumstances.

If we think back upon the previous "Fear not!" statements most have been God calling his servants to stand fast so He could demonstrate His power and will. We may consider Moses standing with Israel on the edge of the sea with the full Egyptian army closing in. "And Moses said to the people, 'Fear not, stand firm, and see the salvation of the LORD, which he will work for you today. For the Egyptians whom you see today, you shall never see again. The LORD will fight for you, and you have only to be silent.'"

This sheds some light as well on the connection between fearless living and God's presence. In the current "Fear not!" Paul is told that the Lord is with him. Perhaps it is within reason to construct the opposite idea: if you are afraid, and God does not tell you (directly or through His word) to "Fear not!" then God is not "with you" – that is, His will is not for you to stay where you are. The correct path is then the one which gets you out of where you are and moves you on. Of course, one might ask how this meshes with Jesus teaching us to not fear those who can only harm the body. If we recall, that teaching referred to the fear of eternal destruction, not simply physical. In the present case, Paul, clearly not fearing any man for he knew God held his eternal soul, nevertheless feared death because it would end his ministry prematurely and therefore he moved on many times.

Prayer: Talk with your Father in heaven about moving on.

Diving In

Read, at a minimum, Acts 18:1-11

Saul.

Once fearlessly complicit in the murder of a follower of Jesus and thereafter ruthlessly pursuing them, this man turned in a very short period of time from being hunter to being hunted by his own people. A single physically, emotionally and spiritually jarring experience with Jesus transformed this man from enemy to advocate, from fanatic hater to fanatic follower.

Saul struck an emotional cord in everyone he encountered. He preached boldly in the name of Jesus and so convinced many of his sincerity. But he also confounded his former friends, scared those he once tried to imprison, and disputed his cause so well that people tried to kill him.

Because his life was threatened in Damascus, those who believed that Saul had been transformed by Jesus secretly took him to Jerusalem. It did not take long for those in Jerusalem to also want to kill Saul, so he escaped again, this time to Tarsus. Later in Antioch, after a period of prayer, worship, and fasting, Saul was set aside by God for the work which God had called him to do.

Question
1. What were Saul's fears?
2. Did Saul live a fearless life in the Lord?
3. How does the radical change in Saul impact the story of your life?

58

Acts 27:24 "Fear not, you must stand before Caesar."

Read first: Acts 27:13-37

Out of the frying pan and into the fire. This old aphorism describes Paul's experience so well. Out of the frying pan of being a prisoner aboard a sinking ship and into the fire of the palace of the king of the pagan Roman Empire. This was Paul's dreaded destiny. Of course Paul saw it differently. He believed he was going from a local mission field ministry to the greatest evangelistic opportunity of all time. Oh, to have Paul's perspective every day in our life!

Paul's perspective on his circumstances was governed by another statement he made to his shipmates, " . . . the God to whom I belong and whom I worship". Paul didn't know the future (until the angel told him) but he did know where he stood at the present moment. He was owned by his Lord Jesus and he worshiped, prayed to, communicated with, preached for, and sang about Him. Sure, Paul had his day job as a tent maker, but he had his life to live as an apostle of the Lord. This life brought with it challenges – some which needed divine intervention to keep the eyes focused on the overall mission.

Perhaps the richest part of this "Fear not!" is that Paul understood God's word as not just for him but for everyone else as well. This was true with Joshua, Hezekiah, and the disciples. God tends to communicate with one person who then is expected to communicate the message to many. Perhaps this method is based on the experience at Mt. Sinai where the people requested God speak to just Moses instead of everyone. Or perhaps it is simply that the best way to learn something is to teach it. This is a marvelous possibility to consider – if we teach a fearless life we may just learn to live one.

Prayer: Talk with your Father in heaven about teaching the fearless life.

> "Yet I see the heterodox assailing the holy Church of God in these days, under the pretence of higher wisdom, and bringing forward works in many volumes in which they offer expositions of the evangelical and apostolic writings, and I fear that if I should be silent and should not put before our members the saving and true doctrines, these teachers might get a hold of curious souls, which, in the absence of wholesome nourishment, might go after food that is forbidden, and, in fact, unclean and horrible."
> – Origen, Commentary on John, Book V

Diving In

Read, at a minimum, Acts 27:13-37

Paul.

Paul was not well-liked. Three times he was beaten with rods. Once he was stoned – so badly everyone thought he was dead. At least three times people plotted and tried to kill him. Crowds were turned against him in Thessalonica, Lystra, Iconium, Philippi, Thessalonica, Berea and Corinth.

Paul had a very rough life. Three times he was shipwrecked. He spent a day and a night adrift on the sea. He was in danger from robbers and natural forces. He had many sleepless nights and was often hungry. He was imprisoned many times and faced a constant and unnamed 'thorn in the flesh' which, despite his pleading, was not taken away by Jesus.

Paul was also a prolific speaker and writer. He planted numerous churches. He converted countless men and women. He shared Jesus with the Jew and the Greek, the slave and the free, the rich and the poor, with anyone who would listen and with many who refused.

The last note that the Bible records about Paul is that he was living in his own rented house in Rome, preaching and teaching about Jesus Christ.

Question
1. What were Paul's fears?
2. Did Paul live a fearless life in the Lord?
3. How does his career impact the story of your life?

59

Revelation 1:17 "Fear not, I am the first and the last."

Read first: Revelation 1:9-20

It is round two for John the disciple; first on the high mountain, now on the island of Patmos. The first time obviously didn't soften the blow of the unveiled Christ. As with the men before him, John falls down as if dead and is subsequently touched and told to "Fear not!"

The vision of Jesus and resulting explanation gives some reason why John should "Fear not!" What John sees is not the Jesus he knew on earth; it is in fact barely a man. White hair, eyes of fire, feet of glowing metal, roaring voice, sword flying out of the mouth and a face like staring into the sun – enough to strike fear in the most stouthearted man. Then the man/son of man speaks and defines, or helps put into perspective, what John is seeing. This awesomeness is the first and the last. This mind-boggling figure is a living being. This glowing, blazing, light-emitting robed and sashed son of man holds the power to confine death and hell. In other words, John may "Fear not!" because what he sees is forever, all-powerful, Life. This is far beyond anything John could have imagined but that does not necessitate that it be something untoward.

Man was made in the image of God, not as a duplicate of God or of an angel. We live in a created world designed for us, we do not live in the heaven suited for God and his hosts. Neither are we privy to see the other world, the other level of existence, except on rare occasions. Due to its stunning differences, we are apt to feel afraid, inferior, and downright mortal when it is revealed. It is the words "Fear not!" which bridge this gap between the earthly and the heavenly, between the moral and the immortal. The rest of the vision of John should be read with this in mind. What is revealed is fantastic, sometimes terrible, sometimes incomprehensible, but it is nevertheless a glimpse into the will of the Eternal One and into how the Eternal One wishes us to see all of existence.

Prayer: Ask your Father in heaven to encourage you that what is to come is far greater than we expect or can imagine.

Diving In

Read, at a minimum, Revelation 1:9-20

John.

He saw Jesus transfigured, betrayed, crucified, risen, ascended to heaven and revealed in heavenly glory.

He is described as being the disciple whom Jesus loved.

It was said of him that if it was the will of Jesus that he live until Jesus came again, that no one should be concerned about that.

He was given the revelation of the future.

He wrote the most famous Bible verse of all time: For God so loved the world, that he gave his only begotten Son, that whoever believes in him should not perish, but have everlasting life.

He wrote: God is love.

Question
1. What were John's fears?
2. Did John live a fearless life in the Lord?
3. How does John's varied life and writings impact the story of your life?

60

Revelation 2:10 "Fear not what you are about to suffer."

Read first: Revelation 2:8-11

This last "Fear not!" in the Bible falls in line with Matthew 10:26 and 28. It is a blessing to know ahead of time that you are to be tested, that there is a time limit to the suffering, and that faithfulness results in eternal life. This scenario has such great similarities to Jesus own life and death where he promised (prophesied) that he would suffer and die and on the third day rise from the dead.

It is to some fairly destitute people that this word of God comes. They are already persecuted, already poor, already reviled. Now things are going to get worse. So, this was probably not what the church members wanted to hear. There was no, "Life is going to get better." or "God will eliminate your enemies." or "You'll end up just like Job with many children and a happy home." Instead these men and women probably left sons and daughters as orphans, left other Christians wondering if it was all worth it, and left the evil pagans feeling secure in their wickedness. It doesn't seem fair when you look at it in this way.

But God didn't ask them to care about these matters – just their own faithfulness. They had to trust that their children would be cared for by the heavenly Father, that the faith of others would be a nurtured by the Faith-Giver, that the wicked would be blown away as chaff at the proper time. Their care and concern was fearless living in the face of permitted evil; their strength and hope had to be in the One who promised the crown of life. May all such martyrs of our Lord be faithful unto the end!

Prayer: Talk with your Father in heaven being fearless and faithful unto the end.

> "Do not then let us consent to perish together with such sinners. Let us fear the awful judgment. Let us keep before our eyes the terrible day of the retribution of the Lord. Let us not consent to perish in other men's sins."
> – Basil, Letter CCXVII

Diving In

Read, at a minimum, Revelation 2:8-11

Timothy.

To the apostle Paul, Timothy was a joy. Paul describes Timothy as "my fellow worker", a "servant of Jesus Christ", "my true child in the faith", "my beloved child" and "our brother".

Two letters written by Paul to Timothy are preserved in the Scriptures and each has the tone of a loving father speaking to a dear son. Paul writes to Timothy that he should, "not be ashamed", "do your best", "flee youthful passions", "do not rebuke an older man", "continue in what you have learned", "let no one look down on you because of your age", and "preach the word". Paul also says, "I remember your tears. . . I long to see you." and "Do your best to come to me soon."

Having been circumcised by Paul, having proclaimed the word of God alongside of Paul, having been sent by Paul as a witness and teacher, and having co-authored letters to the new Christian churches, Timothy is set before all Christians as a believer who truly feared Jesus our Lord.

Question
1. What were Timothy's fears?
2. Did Timothy live a fearless life in the Lord?
3. How does his career impact the story of your life?

CONCLUSIONS

I have been very blessed by the study of the Bible's "Fear not!" commands. I hope you have as well. Probably most surprising to me was the depth and variety of situations and meanings which I discovered. In retrospect I believe I was under the mistaken impression that the "Fear not!" commands were straight forward, simple even. After a year of study I again see how much greater my God is than I imagined.

So what is fearless living? Fearless living describes the kind of life, perspective and heart that God our Father wants for his children. It is not a life void of fear. It is not a life filled with fear. God's vision and desire for us is to have us first understand that fear is something that He created us with. Fear can warn us and keep us safe. Fear can also set up a proper attitude and approach to God. Second, God wants us to understand that fear is properly managed, or focused, or placed, under his guidance and direction. One reason He says "Fear Not!" so many times in the Bible is to make us aware of when we are unbalanced in our fear. Another reason is to teach us that He is aware of when and why we fear. A third reason is to remind us and teach us how we may properly have no fear in many situations and have great fear in others. Finally, God's vision and desire for us is to increase our faith, trust and reliance upon Him and Him alone.

While there are many lessons that God teaches through his "Fear not!" commands, here are seven which I found to be very helpful. 1) To fear is human. 2) We fear the future, and each other, more than anything. 3) God cares about all measure of fears. 4) The Divine is a very scary presence. 5) The opposite of fear is trust. 6) The key reason to "Fear not!" is God's presence. 7) To live a "Fear not!" life requires an adjustment of perception.

1. To fear is human.

As I began this study I speculated that fear was wrong; that the reason God kept telling us to "Fear not!" was because we were doing something, or feeling something, that was sinful. However, God created us with the ability, I might even say the necessity, to fear. In our sinful state the rampant expression of fear in our lives prompts God to tell us to "Fear not!" But this command should not be understood as "Stop fearing!" but rather "Fear the right things!" Since fear is a created characteristic, we see that we will either fear something/someone or we will fear God.

If we fear something in this world, we might be fearing with a kind of tunnel vision. When we have tunnel vision fear we fail to see God's presence and deliverance. Thus we need his strong word of "Fear not!" to pull us out of the tunnel and into His light. We can, of course, properly fear something that is in this world, because there are evil and scary things all around us, but only to the extent that we use this fear wisely.

If we are fearing the Uncreated One, we are afraid because His holiness so far surpasses our sinful mortal nature that we fall down fearing His righteous judgment and pleading for His mercy and grace. When we have the fear of God, both fear of his wrath and respectful fear, we are as we should be – repentant and reverent. In our sinful condition, we need the strong word to "Fear not!" so what we may be brought to the mercy and forgiveness of God.

In summary, fear is not a sin; to fear is human. Fearing in the right way is a lifelong process guided by the One who knows no fear.

2. We fear the future, and each other, more than anything.

I charted various aspects of each "Fear not!" passage and discovered that no one in the Bible fears that their 'past will come back to haunt them' so much so that God needs to speak to them about their fear. Certainly there are times when people do fear their past in this way – the brothers of Joseph are a prime example. But never does God address someone afraid of a past action. Instead, the majority of fears are about the future (roughly two-thirds). The rest of the fears are about the present; that is, something happening immediately and not in a real or imagined future. I also discovered that people fear each other more than any other thing (roughly sixty percent). The second most feared thing/person is God (roughly twenty percent).

Sadly, when God comes to say "Fear not!" to one human who is afraid of the other it never is to suggest that the other person isn't scary after all. (I say 'sadly' because it would seem preferable for God to say that evil people do not exist.) Instead God comes to foretell his deliverance and his salvation from evil people. Obviously, people are fully capable of (and are permitted to do) horrible evil. In a somewhat similar vein, when God comes to say "Fear not!" to a person afraid of an angel, it never is to suggest that the Divine isn't scary after all. Instead God comes to offer peace, mercy and grace.

The rest of the "Fear not!" commands are present in an assortment of contexts, namely fearing barrenness, idols, or lack of love.

3. God cares about all measure of fears.

God cares about our personal fears, about love, about fathers, about women, about the land, about animals, and about his people. I am amazed and humbled at God's thorough approach to our fears. He truly wants us to live fearlessly in every aspect of our lives. To help us in this he offers his presence, his vision, his promises, his deliverance, his mercy. Where God is there is no fear unless it is to fear and respect him. God desires us to fear in a healthy way and so he continually prescribes the medicine of trust in his word which says, "Fear not!" God our Father is literally, and spiritually, 'in touch' with us. He knows our secret fears, our expressed fears and even knows about fears which we may have in the future. These 60 devotions on "Fear not!" reveal God's perpetual and persistent care and concern for his children.

4. The Divine is a very scary presence.

Nearly every time an angel shows up, it is a very scary encounter. Where and when God chooses to reveal himself there is mind numbing and/or body crunching fear. In order for God to speak through his messengers, they often have to say, "Fear not!" and then pick their listener up from the ground. In these situations where God is present, the message to "Fear not"! is a synonym for mercy and grace so that the mortal does not need to fear their potential destruction any longer. (This lesson should not be confused with the false idea that now that Jesus has come we no longer need to fear God or false the idea that we are free to waltz into the throne room of God with any and every thought and notion. The coming of Jesus, his total work of salvation for us, his presence at the right hand of the Father, in no way negates the fact that God cannot abide with sin. God, Father and Son and Holy Spirit, will judge and bring judgment upon sin and evil just as it is foretold in the Bible. It is with the sacrifice of Christ Jesus in mind, and the fact of the coming judgment that we even have the seed of the idea that we may approach God in heaven. God the Father, in all his perfection and holiness, is approachable only through the mercy and grace and presence of Jesus. We approach our heavenly Father because we trust in Jesus. What do we trust in Jesus for? We trust that Jesus will remove our sin so that God will hear us. Let us never forget that in our sinful state we may not stand in heaven or approach the throne of God. Once we are relieved of this burden we will then see our Father face to face.)

5. The opposite of fear is trust.

One dictionary states that antonyms for fear are: courage, security, calm, liking, fondness, penchant, predilection. Clearly not a book which uses the Bible for definitions, this dictionary totally missed the antonym of trust. This is how God wants us to understand fear: it is the antithesis of trust. Whether we are fearing man, the future, the present or Himself, God desires us to trust Him for provision and protection. When we trust God there is no need to fear, either things created or uncreated, visible or invisible, real or imagined. Those who trust in God know he is their help and shield and strength. They are "like a tree planted by water, that sends out its roots by the stream, and does not fear when heat comes, for its leaves remain green, and is not anxious in the year of drought, for it does not cease to bear fruit." A fearless life is a life of trust; a life where we do not lean on our own understanding but instead lean on the everlasting Rock which is God. God surrounds those who trust him with love, blessing and enrichment.

6. The key reason to "Fear not!" is God's presence.

God loves to say, "Fear not! For I am with you!" – as if this solves every problem and cures every ill. And from God's point of view it does! God believes (knows) our fears are often so small and inconsequential. He knows that we magnify things and sometimes fall into the temptation of thinking God cannot (or will not) do all he promises. Like a parent comforting a young child by simply 'being there' so too does God our Father desire to assuage our fears though his presence. In fact, just last night (as I write this) my young son simply wanted to hold my hand in the dark of the night. Doing so erased his anxiety, calmed his fears and allowed him to sleep in peace. When I am afraid, and I will be from time to time, I must remember that my Father in heaven wishes to hold me close. Oh, that I would not struggle to escape his strong arms but rest content in his love.

7. To live a "Fear not!" life requires an adjustment of perception.

The lesson with the broadest impact is perception adjustment. People of faith, who continue in faith, move from viewing the world with mortal eyes to eyes of faith. The eyes of faith not only see beyond the moment, they begin to see the meaning of moments. The eyes of faith see wickedness surrounding the righteous as opportunities for God to demonstrate his deliverance. The eyes of faith see the unknown as a path not traveled alone but a path traveled with God. The eyes of faith place the passing glories of fame and fortune next to the unsurpassed glories of eternal existence and are not swayed by the temporary but drawn toward the permanent. The eyes of faith, while aware of the multitude of anxieties, worries, and fears of this earth, look not to how the human can solve every problem and mystery, but look to God for his wisdom and strength. The eyes of faith are not troubled by the inevitable conclusion to this life, also known as death, applying themselves instead to the relationship they have with the One who preserves the soul.

The honest truth is that both the believer and the unbeliever witness and experience the same earthly life. We are born, we grow, we watch others die, we face death ourselves. We get sick, we hunger, we enjoy, we rejoice. Each of us hears the news of wars and natural disasters. Everyone is lied to, cheated, distrusted, and misinformed. We are all sinful and struggle with lust, deception, pride, ambition and embarrassment. Every human life is much the same in these ways. The great difference is having One tell us that there is a different perception of existence, and having that One teach us how He views us and how we should view ourselves.

"Because we have the mercy of this One, we do not lose heart. We have renounced disgraceful, underhanded ways. We refuse to walk in craftiness or to tamper with God's word, but by the open statement of the truth we would ask everyone to consider what He has to say. If any one's mind is darkened to Him, then the god of this world has blinded their minds to keep them from seeing the light of the gospel of the glory of Christ. For this message and this teaching is not from ourselves, but Jesus Christ as Lord. For God, who said, 'Let light shine out of darkness,' has shone in our hearts to give the light of the knowledge of the glory of God in the face of Jesus Christ." (Paraphrase of 2 Corinthians 4:1-6)

Imagine standing in front of a person and the only light source is behind them. You would see nothing but a black shape. But if the light moves to behind you, you may now see that the shape is actually far more than you could have thought possible. This is analogous to how God works. His light shines in such a way as to give us a view of reality far beyond what we thought possible given only the muddled image this world offers. So many of the "Fear not!" statements are the light of God shining bright for us on the events of this life. "Fear not!" those who wish you harm because in God's light they are revealed to have little power. "Fear not!" the future you imagine because in God's light you see how

God has it all working to his glory and our blessing. "Fear not!" the things of this life – food and clothing – because in God's light it is revealed that these are the smallest parts of what he has to give to his children.

Perception adjustment changes how we feel, think, react, plan, pray, teach, learn, grow, and sleep at night. Faith gives strength and hope when it is the filter through which all of life is passed.

ABOUT THE AUTHOR

Timothy Sternberg is blessed by the Lord with his wife Allison and four growing boys. Previously the pastor of congregations in Texas and California, he currently teaches and mentors the Christian faith daily in person and on-line. Timothy often teams up with Allison to lead church retreats. Together, the family enjoys signing and working, camping and bike riding. They currently reside in Central Oregon.